With
Best wishes
in ~~your~~ writing
painting & all
creative adventures!

Minhaj Arifin
April 2014

The characters in this book are purely fictional.
Any similarities between them and real individuals are purely coincidental.

ISBN: 0983863016
ISBN 13: 9780983863014

Table of Contents

Introduction

Desis (they-sees) is the name given to people who migrate to America from India, Pakistan, Bangladesh, Nepal, Sri Lanka, Afghanistan, Middle East, China, Russia, and Antarctica. Desis are the greatest nation on Earth. The evidence of this is present in holy books, prophecies and now scientists as well admit this. But my aim is not to make a case for something so obvious but to explain, in an easy-to-read book, the origins of the Desis. Who are we? As a right-hand man to our great leader Adnan Raheem Khan, I had access to his diary and his personal notes, and I was witness to the many amazing events mentioned in this book. I now reveal to you the story of his leadership and the adventures of our Desi nation. There will be times when readers might feel, "What the hell is this guy saying?" I hope they will overcome those feelings and continue to read the book with their beautiful eyes. And now the story...

Treacherous Mir

"But will I not be despised?"

1757

WHO WAS Mir? Let's just say that he is clearly the most despised man in the history of Desis. In the eighteenth century, the British had hired designers to make evil designs on the Indian subcontinent. The British were powerful and commanded a great and modern army. But a strong Indian king stood up to the British forces, giving them a hard time.

This Indian king had made Mir a general in his army. But even this honor was not enough for the ambitious Mir. He wanted to wear the crown so that everyone would call him "your highness." At the time the Indian king was at war with the British, Mir decided to use this conflict for his own gains. Mir met secretly with Robert Clive, the British officer who wanted to rule India. Robert Clive, dressed in his red coat and long black boots, arrived on his horse for this meeting, bringing a few officers with him.

1

Mir was dressed in royal robes, with a necklace of rare pearls around his neck. His long golden Indian coat shimmered in the orange light of the setting sun. An elephant stood behind him along with several men to guard him against danger.

Robert Clive greeted Mir with great respect. "Greetings, Your Highness."

Though this delighted Mir, he responded with cunning. "I am not king, but a servant to my king."

"Perhaps we can change that together," said Clive getting straight to the point.

"How would we do that?" asked Mir.

"Simple. When we go to war against your king, you must hold back your forces, so that we can crush him!"

Mir looked at the gold-blue sky covered with white clouds. "But will I not be despised?"

"Yes, you will be hated and your name will become synonymous with treachery. You will be to the Desis what Satan is to the religious. In history your name will mean bad things."

"But in my own life? Will I have the kingdom?"

"Indeed. You shall have all the worldly comforts. Inside your palace it will always be India. Women will continue to dance for you and feed you grapes as you recline on comfortable cylindrical pillows with green velvet covers and golden ribbons. Peacocks will roam your palace grounds and all men around you shall call you king."

"And our children? What about our children?"

"Your children shall study in English schools. Frankly, there is going to be a lot of confusion in the next three hundred years. Kids who look Indian will grow up reading English stories about talking rabbits. You are going to have Christmas parties, and fat men will dress up in red suits pretending they are on the North Pole."

"Why will such terrible things happen to our people?"

"It's simple. We have hired designers. And we have the most evil designs. We will crush the spirit of the Desis. There is nothing you can do about this. There is nothing for you to fight for. You don't even know who you are. Who are you?"

"Yes. Who are we?"

Robert Clive smiled and proudly summed up the differences. "Whereas we are a nation united under one language, one fish that we eat with chips, you are a confused people divided into Hindus, Buddhists, Muslims. And even these are divided into Shia, Sunni, Brahmans. Can you even eat together without getting over-excited over one thing or another? It's so difficult to hang out with you guys."

"Yes. This is most true."

"So you see my dear Mir, English victory over the Desis is written not by the sword but by your own history, by your own behavior towards one another."

"Yes, we are a lost cause. I will betray my king. I shall be the dagger in his back. What else do you offer?"

"We will give you lots of tea."

"With milk?"

"That will be up to you. In some cultures they go milk free; personally I don't like that at all."

"I accept and pledge myself to you."

And this is how the great betrayal happened. On the day of battle the Indian king was winning, but Mir told his troops to stand back. The treacherous Mir and his troops stood by as the British defeated the Indian forces. The Indian king lost the battle and along with it the hopes of a great and united Desi nation perished.

Haunted Man

"Okay, so what have you done?"

November 13th, 2008

ADNAN RAHEEM Khan, a man of great mental beauty, lived in Dallas, Texas. In every way you would think him to be normal. His decent mother, his proper wife, Naureen, the two lively children, Bubloo and Tina, the sturdy, dependable Japanese car, and the respectable job at an IT company.

Today as he drove from work on Highway 635 he felt that feeling again—as if he were a child who accompanies his mother to the supermarket and sits in the car-shaped shopping trolley turning the steering wheel furiously but suspecting that he is not in complete control. And this feeling was always followed by the same two questions. *Is this it? Is this life?*

Adnan Raheem Khan sensed a destiny. He may have felt this strongly because of his family background. He was royalty. The framed paintings of his earliest ancestors hung in the hallway of his house. The first painting was of a single cell—the first cell that swam in the ocean. His name was Cellular Khan. Adnan was his direct descendent.

The second oil painting was also of a single cell, green in color, titled "Chlorophyll Khan." Chlorophyll Khan was the first cell that succeeded in obtaining energy from the sun. His historic achievement led to the release of oxygen in the atmosphere creating an environment that would further the cause of all living things by allowing them to breath and eat.

The third painting displayed another illustrious ancestor: Multi-Cellular Khan. It was he who had suggested for the first time that cells should join together to form higher life-forms such as fish. The great architect of unity is responsible for all complex life as we know it.

The fourth painting was titled "Sir Millipede Khan the First." He was the first sea creature to crawl out of the ocean and onto land. The large framed painting showed this great ancestor leaving the ancient, blue-green ocean and placing his first foot on land.

It is said that Sir Millipede Khan became emotional at this moment. "Finally we will have peace. None of that ocean nonsense where creatures eat each other." He was an optimist, a pioneer embodying the spirit of the immigrant who finds hope in a new place.

He was eaten.

The next painting displayed Sir Ape Khan walking on two feet. This action left his hands free to do things. It was a profound moment. Reliable sources confirm that he said, "Now that our hands are free we will make this earth a paradise. We shall use our hands to applaud one another. This will boost our self-esteem, and joy will fill our hearts." Under the beautiful large green tree, which also served as the first science lab, Sir Ape Khan would go on to create the first stick. It did not involve much work, as the stick was actually a branch that fell from the tree. But it was a beginning and Sir Ape Khan, Adnan's great ancestor, had started it.

Further down the hall were paintings of other illustrious ancestors such as Alexander the Great, Cleopatra, Asoka, and many other kings and emperors. But for the year 1700, an empty frame hung on this wall of great ancestors. Why was this frame empty? The dark reason was that Adnan's great-great-great-grandfather was the treacherous Mir. And so Adnan, who could trace his ancestry back to the greatest of kings was unfortunately related to the one man every Desi despised. This bothered Adnan, and sometimes he wanted to shout out to the world, "Yes I am the great-great-great-grandson of Mir. So what?"

But he kept this a secret and he tried his best to be normal like everyone else. Flossing his teeth, buying massive quantities of liquid soap, watching reality show marathons and using cake mixes to bake tasty things and feel good about himself. But this secret ancestor haunted him. When he walked through that hallway he would glance at that empty frame and fall into a dark mood. He would retreat to his computer den, which he had converted into his private office by closing off the entrance with a shower curtain. Just outside this office, Adnan had installed a red bulb on the ceiling. When the red bulb was lit, it meant that absolutely no one in the house was allowed to disturb him. Sadly, no one complied with this strict law.

Inside the office was a large sturdy desk and behind it on the wall, a map of the world. Here he would drown himself in sorrow, looking at the world map and singing songs from the eighties. On his desk was a large phone, not the piece of plastic trash we see these days, cordless and shameless, but an actual phone like they had back in the eighties. It had a dial, in which the finger may be inserted and a manly call be made to someone.

Adnan felt the burden of history. His ancestors, who had given the world oxygen, inspired other cells to combine and form higher life forms, discovered land, now looked down on him from the windows of paradise and asked, "Okay, so what have you done?" Sometimes this feeling got to be too much for Adnan and he looked for a way out—or for a mentor, someone who knew the answer to the great questions of life. And so he had been corresponding with Hercules. He wrote long letters in deep-green ink with a fountain pen on beautiful papyrus-colored paper. Today he had written these words:

> *Dear Hercules,*
> *It seems to me that it is only you who has not compromised. Everyone else must negotiate with joy. They place hurdles before themselves. But you live naked and free. Truly you are an example for mankind.*

Just as he was signing his name to this letter, his wife, Naureen, pushed aside the plastic curtain and entered, ignoring the red light bulb, which was lit and signaled the need for extreme privacy. Their conversation would change the destiny of our nation.

"It was alive"

N AUREEN HAD grown up in Karachi, Pakistan, where she attended a girl's convent school. In this school are found statues of Jesus Christ, heavy iron and wood furniture, tiled floors that resemble marble chessboards, piano-playing Catholic nuns, and a history dating back to 1862. This great institution with its Gothic buildings became known for its chili chips, corn dipped in spicy liquids, and the independent attitudes of its students. It was in this complex environment that Naureen had grown up, experimenting with different flavors of lip gloss, singing songs by British pop stars, and playing hopscotch, a complicated game that involves jumping, turning, and throwing. By the time she was ten she could draw portraits of all her teachers in cartoon format. At sixteen, she entered college, and it was there that she felt an immense desire to help humans in some medical manner. And so she studied biology, learning all there was to know about the anatomy of frogs.

By the age of eighteen she was dating a boy from college. They walked on the beach, eating peanuts and discussing in detail their horoscopes. Naureen kept her boyfriend a secret as girls in Pakistan often do. When Naureen was twenty-one, her mother received a marriage proposal for her from the Khan family. Adnan, who had just finished his master's degree in computer science and was well settled in the United States, was considered a good catch in Karachi. Naureen and Adnan met at a Chinese restaurant, where Adnan told her that the fall of the Berlin Wall would change everything. While she considered him to be boring, Naureen also felt safe in this man's presence. When Manchurian chicken was served and sweet-and-sour prawns emitted a delicious steamy smoke, Adnan asked, "Naureen, will you marry me this December because it fits my work schedule?" She said yes. At the time it seemed like the right thing to do. And right things often get boring. Now, fifteen years later, they were unhappily married with two extremely happy children.

"The Shaans are coming over for dinner tonight. Make sure you vacuum the carpet in the living room," said Naureen mechanically.

Adnan was in no mood for visitors, especially the Shaans. "Why do we have to invite them? Didn't we just visit them last Friday?"

"Which is all the more reason to invite them for dinner. We have to maintain strategic balance."

"We work so hard to remain unhappy!"

"Don't start right now. Just do your part. We'll talk about this later."

Adnan looked deeply into the shower curtain. "I am going to Africa. I have a meeting with Hercules."

"Are you crazy? Do you know that the kids have to go to school tomorrow and that you have to drop them, so that they can gain an education and do the same thing for their kids?"

"Yes, but I am sick of this cycle."

"What cycle?"

"This life cycle of a mosquito."

"What do you mean? You are not a mosquito. You are a computer engineer who solves problems for a network of computers. When e-mails are lost or deleted by mistake you restore them."

"I am tired of all this, Naureen! I remember reading about the life cycle of a mosquito. He comes into this world and hangs around damp areas where still water is available, and then in just five days, he dies. No one cares for him. We don't even give him a name. He is called the mosquito."

"So?"

"It's so generic. It's like me calling you woman. It's offensive. Don't you get it? It's alive! For our science class I had to draw him with a pencil. There was all this fuss about anterior angle and dorsal view. But who really gave a damn about his feelings?"

"He is a mosquito! What does that have to do with your life?"

"It does, Naureen. Just like the mosquito dies after five days so do I work from nine to five. And every day I die at work doing something I hate. This is not what I had in mind when I was growing up, when I walked over to Abbasi."

"What was Abbasi?"

"It was a small shop, and a guy named Abbasi owned it. He did not even have a regular fridge. He kept ice in a box, in which he stored bottles of cold orange soda, and when he reached in to grab the cold glass bottles they collided with each other in the freezing water and melting ice, making the sounds of heaven."

"Makes sense, but still irrelevant," she said like a judge who is also a wife.

"At Abbasi's I would pay eight rupees for a tennis ball and perhaps five rupees for an electric tape. And that tape I wrapped around the tennis ball so that it bounced better. We played cricket till the sun went down. We played real cricket. Not for money or fame or popularity. The real cricket! We drank orange soda, and the sun and I were friends because she made me sweaty and red and brown and happy."

"You are weird," said Naureen. She was not supporting him through this conversation.

But Adnan had more to add. "I wanted to be a knight in shiny silver armor. I wanted to help children, do something for human rights. But instead I am surrounded by people who are guarding me against having a life."

"Oh, so you think we are a burden on you! Do you know that I made a sacrifice by marrying you? Many were the men who wanted my hand in marriage, but I gave them no thought and ignored all the letters of love they sent me. I can prove it, because I got them laminated and I keep them organized in alphabetical order for easy access on lonely nights."

Adnan then put his mug on the table. And guess what? He didn't use the coaster—the disk on which beverages are placed to prevent stains on the table.

"*Put the coaster under the mug*," she said harshly. "*You will stain the table.*"

At this moment, Adnan realized that he couldn't compromise with the coaster, because in his heart he knew that the coaster was something abnormal. As a modern, rational man he could not live with this stupidity. Why was the table created? So that we could put things on it. The coaster was irrelevant and only the force of tradition kept it alive in households all over the world. He knew this. The time had come to fight for what was right.

"Naureen," he said, "We protect the table from the mug by placing the coaster in between. But the table was bought with the intention of keeping things on it. And yet the coaster is used to protect the table from the very thing it was meant to do. I don't think I need to use the coaster."

Naureen's eyes turned dinosaur green with anger. "How dare you! Are we to become animals and put mugs full of water upon tables without the use of coasters? What is next?"

"This" said Adnan, picking up the coaster and throwing it like a small frisbee into the trash bin. He then walked out of his house, got into in his car, and drove to the Dallas airport. He was coming to Africa.

"He stood at the entrance of a cave"

THE ACTUAL location of Hercules remains a secret and this writer will not betray the lord of strength by revealing it. Following the map Hercules had included in his letters, Adnan reached a great waterfall. The map instructed, "When you reach the waterfall, just go in it." Adnan walked into the thick wall of water. The water crashed on him, pushing him down as he moved forward slowly. Suddenly, the water was behind him and he stood at the entrance of a cave. For a few seconds he hesitated, but the loud thrashing water behind him encouraged him to walk forward into this cave of mystery. He entered the cave and walked into a tunnel filled only with darkness. He walked for some time. The low roof above disappeared, and he was standing inside a hollow mountain lit with the brilliance of a thousand lamps. Everywhere he looked he saw light, and there was no turning away from it. A voice boomed like the sound of thunder in this cave of light.

"Why do you come here?"

"I am Adnan Raheem Khan."

"Why should we allow you in our world?"

"I seek wisdom..."

13

"Can you be more specific?"

"I am here to see the rainbow of my dreams, I am here to worship all its colors."

The great voice was silent for a moment. And then it spoke. "Okay, weirdo, you can go through."

He kept walking and entered another tunnel that had light at the end of it. He followed this light and finally saw the exit from this large wondrous cave. He climbed out of the tunnel and stood in a jungle among ancient trees. Immediately Adnan knew his place in the family of natural things. He was a child. The trees were the adults. The trunks were massive, their leafy tops talked to the sky allowing the sun only enough room to create pillars of light in this dense jungle.

"Welcome."

Adnan turned around. Standing in the shade of a tree was a muscular being. His wavy black hair had never met a comb. "You are the lord of strength. You are Hercules," said Adnan.

"I am," said Hercules, coming out of the shade. He belonged to nature completely. He was not observing nature with binoculars, his eyes did not hide behind sunglasses, his feet did not reside in hiking shoes. Nature was in his nature. He handed Adnan a coconut. A straw made from a leaf stuck out of it. Adnan took the gift of freshness and sipped the cool coconut milk. It was like discovering liquids for the first time.

"You know I truly admire you," said Adnan.

"Is it because I walk with lions, swim with sharks, and tease alligators?"

"Yes, all those things, and also you have never compromised. You wear lion-skin underwear and you are completely okay with this."

"What's underwear?"

Adnan pointed to the lion hide Hercules wore around his waist.

"Oh, I usually go without that," said Hercules. "I only wear it on formal occasions. I knew you were coming to visit, so I wore this, for I know people from your world are most uptight."

"I really appreciate it," said Adnan. "But your wife, Sheeba, doesn't mind you going around naked?"

"No, she likes it. The jungle wants us to be naked. Anyone in too much clothing is considered an embarrassment here. Sheeba and I, we want to blend in as much as possible. We try not to stand out here."

"Yours was a marriage made in heaven," said Adnan smiling in wonder.

Hercules laughed. "I know the rumor in the jungle is, oh, it was love at first sight, it was meant to be, it's just right, but even before Sheeba, I fell in love many times."

"You did?"

"Of course. It's natural. I met a beautiful giraffe at a dance party. She had the longest legs, and I loved that about her. Our relationship was mostly physical. The fascination faded quickly."

"Why?"

"We never saw eye to eye. I then dated an octopus for a while. She was really smart but demanding. Whenever we went out she always wanted me to hold her hand, and my thing was, okay, which one? Finally when Sheeba came along, lightning struck."

"Ah yes! True love is like lightning," said Adnan. "How we all wish we could experience that sudden rush of feeling."

"Lightning struck her husband, and she became available. When I first saw her, there she was, using her strong white teeth to break a coconut. And now we are together. We are at a very good place right now."

"Emotionally, you mean?"

"No, geographically," he said and pointed upward to the top of a tree. "That is my summer home. Let me show you."

Hercules climbed the large tree which had grooves made in it. "I made those for Sheeba so she can climb down easily. You can use those to come up."

Adnan followed Hercules up the trunk and, after a lot of climbing, he could see the living space. Rough but charming, it was a large room made of leaves and branches.

"We have a human," shouted Hercules. Adnan entered this house, which was confusing to him because of all the leaves and branches. But as he walked farther, he understood the architecture. The floor was covered with soft grass padding. The roof was made with ropes of flowers, red, yellow, and white. The sun turned the petals into crystals, showering this home with colored light.

"Oh that's lovely," said Sheeba. She was dressed in a grass skirt, her hair was pulled back and held together in a pineapple shell. She wore a necklace of grapes and her teeth were like white pearls. Hercules kissed Sheeba on the stomach. To the sophisticated city folk who shop in stores and eat doughnuts this greeting may have seemed odd, but it made sense at the moment. They were in love.

Hercules pulled away a curtain made from peacock feathers to reveal a view of a magnificent waterfall. Adnan watched the large volume of water slip over the mountain as if in slow motion, falling a thousand feet below to crash into a river, sending up misty vapors that made the leaves wet.

Sheeba made tea, which they sipped from wooden cups. As a guest, Adnan was given the seat of honor, a bed of flowers and leaves, soft and soothing. They sat there watching the hypnotic fall of water as Sheeba served mangoes. Small particles of water slapped their happy faces all day long as they ate fruits and stretched lazily on soft, luxurious leaves. Hours went by and yet they sat in silence.

The jungle, Adnan realized, was not a place for small talk. There was no chitchat about the stock market or how the interest rates were doing in the housing market. No talk about

16

bills, or what credit card was offering zero percent APR. This was the jungle, and no one here gave a flying frisbee about interest rates and credit cards unless they could eat them.

Adnan felt so much at home that he fell asleep. When he woke up from this most peaceful sleep, Hercules was looking at him.

"You are now rested from your journey. Let us walk in the jungle."

They climbed down from this magnificent tree house and strolled in the jungle, which was to Hercules a private and delightful garden, every creature his friend, every plant a comfort.

"Truly, Hercules, your life is happy," said Adnan. "There is no hesitation in your life. Your house is a spa, your wife is in love with you. And you don't get stuck in traffic in the morning."

"What is traffic?"

"Every morning millions of people place themselves in metallic cages that are hurled down the highway in the morning, trying to reach a destination they don't like, and as they get in one another's way they get upset if someone does not allow them to go first. So they honk all the way, an angry mechanical scream, the sound of their anguish. And even when they do reach their place of work, anger is followed by the sadness of doing something they secretly hate, which is followed by the fear of not being allowed to do it, and so they pretend to love everything by the saying of things such as 'ETA,' 'FYI,' 'right away,' 'sure thing,' 'thank you for this opportunity,' and 'I will enjoy overcoming this challenge.'"

"What is a highway?"

It was getting late and Adnan felt for a moment that perhaps this meeting was a mistake. If he could not understand the world Adnan came from, how could Hercules help him? He also worried about getting back to the airport on time. "Do you know what time it is? It's getting late."

"What is time?"

"We have divided the day into numbers that we start counting the moment we wake up."

"Why?"

"So that we are not late for things like work, appointments, meetings, and deadlines." Then Adnan lifted his left hand to show Hercules the digital watch he was wearing. "See, this is the time counter that I wear on my hands. We call it the watch."

"May I have it?" said Hercules.

Adnan took off his watch and gave it to the great man, and then Hercules, lord of strength, king of lions, crushed it with his strong bare hands. A thousand pieces of plastic fell to the ground.

"That was made in Taiwan and I got a good deal at the outlet mall. It had a stopwatch!"

"What is that?"

"It's when we count really fast. It helps us to record our performance and make things efficient."

"The world you come from is a terrible place," said Hercules. "Let me show you." And he took Adnan to the highest mountaintop. From there they could see the whole world as it should be: lush with greenery, peppered with dark trees, with hills like scoops of pistachio ice cream, rivers like sky-blue ribbons sparkling under the glorious African sun, mountain peaks covered with ivory snow that became gold in the morning light, majestic rocks uncut, and a proud sky fragrant with the scent of flowers and fresh leaves.

"This is my world," said Hercules. "Is it not nice?"

"This whole place is an eye freshener!" said Adnan.

The view from the mountain had given Adnan a burst of energy. He was again that child who played cricket under the sun.

"I have to go now," said Adnan.

He remained in a highly positive and creative state of mind as he traveled back from Africa. On the plane he ate roasted peanuts; and I mean he really *ate* them, crunching them with enthusiasm, calling the flight attendant again and again to bring him more. He drank orange juice from a beautiful plastic cup. He drank with the thirst of a man who had reached the end of a great desert and had found a vending machine full of soft drinks. As the plane flew toward America, he looked into the golden African clouds from his window seat. He was so inspired he called the flight attendant again, and when she came to him he whispered into her ear.

"I am reborn. I will change the world."

She called security.

"He was the captain of disobedience"

A DNAN LANDED back in Dallas on Monday at eight in the morning. Instead of going home he went straight to his place of work.

The manager was upset with Adnan because Adnan looked happy. "We need to discuss something. This is very serious."

In the last few years Adnan had become mentally and emotionally detached from work, so in his cubicle he had been writing letters to himself. One of these letters the manager had discovered in the printer.

Dear Adnan,

The only thing giving you satisfaction here is the vending machine that dispenses chocolate muffins. Today they did not even have those. They call you a network engineer, but frankly you have no idea what you are doing here. There are too many buttons on every machine. Every time something goes wrong with the servers, they ask you to fix it. You always apply the same technique. Reboot. When no one is watching, you unplug the machine and then quickly plug it back in. That is what you have been doing for the last five years. One day they will find out. So here you are stuck inside a cement box on a

*beautiful day pretending to know something. Sometimes you
wish you were a cowboy enjoying the wilderness under the open
skies. Anyway do not forget to buy skim milk on the way home.*
   Yours truly, because I am you,
   Adnan Raheem Khan

The manager walked into Adnan's cubicle, which was dec-
orated with posters of leadership personalities such as Nelson
Mandela, Ronald Reagan, and Michael Jackson.

"I found this in the printer," said the manager throwing
the letter on Adnan's desk. For years Adnan had been writing
such things to himself. Letters from the inner being, he liked
to call them. The one person who should not have read this
letter had not only read it but had it in print.

The manager, now aware of the reboot procedure,
demanded an explanation. "What is the meaning of this
letter?"

Adnan looked at the letter; his own thoughts stared back
at him with expectations. He touched the paper with his finger tips. "The meaning, you ask?"

"You are writing offensive letters to yourself in font size
twelve. I want to know the meaning of this."

Before meeting Hercules in Africa, Adnan would have
understood this question as a complaint. But now every word
held a deeper message. What indeed was the meaning of
this letter? "The meaning...the meaning..." repeated Adnan
mostly to himself.

The manager shook his head and spoke in his official,
serious voice. "If your performance does not get better, we
will have to let you go. You really need to get it together."

And then something very normal happened, something
that happens all the time but this time, it would produce
abnormal results. One of Adnan's co-workers, who liked to
do neck yoga, got up and turned the office blinds upward.
In that dull office, with a gray carpeted floor, the sun, from

ninety-three million miles away, sent particles of light that collided and danced on Adnan's skin and fused with his mental beauty. He picked up the wireless keyboard from his desk and threw it on the floor.

"What are you doing? That's expensive equipment!" cried the manager.

All other workers rose in their cubicles to get a view of this action. Secretly they were loving it, because all this was unusual and broke routine. But they made sure that their faces looked worried. Adnan Raheem Khan, descendent of Cellular Khan, leaped onto the chair and then from there jumped onto the desk, standing on it like a king. From there he could see everything. The photocopy machine, the water cooler, the coffee station, the many serious-looking heads that had all turned to see him.

Inhaling deeply he let out the loudest, manliest scream ever heard inside an office building. "*Aaahaaaaaaaaaaaa.*" He also beat his chest like a gorilla.

"What the hell is wrong with him?" said a co-worker, who was excellent in technical support and had dedicated his life to several operating systems.

"I think he ate too many well-preserved doughnuts from the vending machine," said another worker, who spent most of his time playing foosball in the company recreation room.

"I think he is having a heart attack," said another worker, who had wanted to become an archeologist but got pulled into IT because everyone was doing it in the nineties.

"Why do you scream?" asked the manager who had never dealt with this kind of behavior in an indoor environment. There was no user manual or procedure to deal with this.

"I am a free man," said Adnan. "I don't need you, I don't need this job."

"But you have a mortgage and kids and car payments and several bills to think about. How will you pay them if you stop receiving paychecks? It's the circle of life. There are even songs about it in animated movies."

When a man screams that loud, he recalls from his suppressed memory the days of majesty, when he ran with bulls, lived in caves and painted on the walls, hunted large animals by day and roasted them at night. Adnan jumped down from his desk and landed on the floor like a superhero. He reached into his pocket for the flash drive the company had issued him. Throwing it on the ground he crushed it with his feet like a smoker who has had his last cigarette.

"Are you completely crazy?" shouted the manager. "Do you realize that flash drive has eighteen gigabytes? Imagine how many files of data you could have saved on it!"

"I save me! I save me!" shouted Adnan with a faraway look in his eyes. He was smiling, defeating his fears as well as the English language. He was the captain of disobedience and his happy lips were stretched from ear to ear, and his teeth and gums were visible like a confident man in a toothpaste commercial.

"Your behavior is unacceptable. Your happiness is out of control!" shouted the manager.

But Adnan was too far gone now. It was like the first bite into a hot pancake filled with crunchy pecans. Nothing would stop him from getting more of it. And so it was in this new, kingly state of mind that he addressed his manager. "What will you do to me? Will you hold me in chains and whip me? Will you scar my chest with a large knife and make me walk on burning coals?"

"No," said the manager. "We will disable your password and give you a cardboard box in which you can take your things."

Fame

"We have a crazy"

―――――――⋄―――――――

ADNAN FILLED up the cardboard box and walked out of the office building for the last time. As he exited the fluorescent-lit building and stepped outside, he felt the sun on his face. It is true, great men communicate with nature not in English or Italian, but in gratitude.

He opened the door of his car and inhaled deeply. It smelled like wet newspapers and food garbage. Sand from their trip to Galveston beach covered the floor mats. Pizza crusts with teeth marks lay scattered in the back seat. Empty soda cans lay on piles of paper: wrappers from chocolate energy bars, income tax returns, printed maps, and unread magazines. The front passenger seat was filled with computer books that told mankind where to click. The windows of the car were so dirty that they were no longer transparent but had become stained glass in this moving temple of filth.

He went to the back of the office building where mops and cleaning supplies were kept. The manager, who was watching him from the third floor, became concerned and alerted security. Adnan picked up all the things he could find, carpet shampoo, a water hose, scrubbing brushes and liquid soap. He placed these items around his car and, like a general who takes a brave view of the battlefield, he walked around his car

25

examining the tough task ahead. Suddenly he leaped like a tiger and pulled the floor mats out of the car.

The security guards, who have little excitement in their lives, came into the parking lot. "What are you doing?"

"Taking the trash out of my life," said Adnan.

"We want you to leave right now."

"I am not leaving until this car is cleaned."

By now the office workers had gathered behind the security guards. They peeked curiously like children who for the first time were attending a gladiator show in ancient Rome. Adnan used the hose to throw water on his car. The water hit the roof, turning the dirt a darker shade. Some of it splashed into the small crowd of formally dressed workers. Drops of water landed on the feet of a female worker who worked as a project manager. "Oh my God, my shoes!" And yet as she felt the cool water entering her painful high-heeled shoes, she secretly enjoyed it.

"We are calling the police," said the security guard. But he couldn't. The sight of a man cleaning his car after five years was too interesting.

Adnan picked up the mats one by one and slammed them against the concrete floor of the parking lot. Small mushroom clouds of dust surrounded his face. He coughed and continued. He poured the carpet shampoo. The gleaming purple liquid fell like a translucent rope snaking its way into the grooves of the floor mats. Using a large brush with bright yellow bristles, he scrubbed the mats. At first the soapy foam was black, and then gray, and finally there was no dirt left and the foam turned to white. He scrubbed the wheel caps, removing the black oil and grime. One scrub after another, the silver metallic surface emerged from under the dirt. He scrubbed the car on the outside, transforming it from dirt brown to an eggshell white. The windows became transparent again. Then he realized that the back windshield was covered in a dark tint of lamination.

"No, don't even go there!" shouted an ex-co-worker who had become emotionally involved with all this.

"Oh, I will go there," said the great man. He took a blade and scraped the tint slowly. The tint came off in thin strips of gray ugly plastic, one scrape after another until it was all gone. The back windshield became transparent, allowing the sun to enter. After five years the car said "hi, there" to the world of light. Adnan pulled out a car air freshener that he had been saving for the longest time. Soon the car was filled with the fragrance of freshly cut oranges.

Adnan now addressed the workers who stood there hypnotized by this transformation. "The next time you are in your office and you feel that all your gods have abandoned you, that your childhood is over, that the highlight of your day is to drink bad office coffee with that disgusting powdered creamer, your only friend a vending machine, remember this day when a man like you became free."

The workers watched him drive out of the parking lot and out of their lives. Then they went back to work.

Adnan stopped by the convenience store and purchased an extra-large soft drink. As the tasty slushy ice particles landed on his tongue he merged onto Highway 635. He was enjoying even merging into traffic! The most boring thing was giving him joy. On a Monday! Rolling down the windows, he enjoyed the wind hitting his face. He turned on the radio and a lively song filled the air. Science tells us that there are moments in our lives when a random radio song is able to describe, in sound and lyrics, our deepest desires. Adnan pushed the accelerator, feeling the vibrations of the engine through the soles of his affordable shoes. In just five seconds, the car fired into high speed, going from sixty miles an hour to sixty-one miles an hour. After ten minutes he was doing seventy on a highway that did not allow sixty-five. A cop who was on duty and hiding his police car in the cover of bushes saw the shiny white car dash past him like a snow leopard.

The cop, who needed to make his ticket quota for the month, thanked karma because he was a Buddhist, turned on the sirens, and chased Adnan. Adnan saw bright cop-car lights flashing in his rearview mirror. But there was the engine that drove the car and then there was the radio song that drove Adnan.

For five years Adnan had used Highway 635 to drive to work and back. Here on this highway he had gotten tickets for not updating the tags on his car. There was history between 635 and Adnan, and most of it was boring. Today that would change.

"They'll never take me on 635."

With the confidence that comes from not thinking, Adnan turned the steering wheel sharply. At the speed of seventy-five, the car had been moving forward. That's what the accelerator, the engine, momentum, and gravity had been working on as a team. That's what they did everyday. When Adnan turned the steering wheel sharply, the tires turned to the right, and came into conflict with the rest of the car which still wanted to move forward. The car lurched sideways almost horizontally (like a stick figure in a foosball game) crossing two lanes at once, making a mockery of all the things they teach in driving school. The turning tires lost skin to cement, coating the smooth surface of Highway 635 with a slanting line of black rubber. Adnan was in the right lane flooring the accelerator. He was a fugitive.

On normal days Adnan would have first given the indicator. Civilized, blinking, orange lights would have signaled his intention to switch lanes. And then someone nice would have slowed down, allowing Adnan to cautiously switch lanes. Sometimes no one gave him space to change lanes, and he would submissively carry on, driving into exits that took him to cities he had never seen. But today he was an animal hunting joy. Smoke from his hot wheels created a white cloud that told everyone that something special was happening.

All other drivers on the highway slowed down in respect for Adnan and also because they wanted to watch a free show. The cop in pursuit picked up his radio and said the words that are now recorded in history and portrayed in movies all over the world.

"We gotta crazy one! I repeat—we have a crazy..."

By the time the police car made it to the right lane, Adnan was driving in the shoulder of the highway. Next to the highway was a grassy area that merged into a hill. The cop now moved behind Adnan and used loud speakers to warn him.

"Slow down and stop the car right now."

Meanwhile at home, his wife, Naureen, was watching her favorite soap opera. But today the soap was interrupted by a phone call.

It was her neighbor. "Your husband is on TV. Switch to *Hi There News.*"

Naureen switched the channel, and on the screen was a helicopter view of their car speeding down the highway. A close-up shot showed Adnan drinking a large drink while going very fast in the shoulder area.

The live footage was accompanied by these comments:

> *A South Asian man in his forties, who beat his chest at work and then quit, is now being chased by state troopers for speeding and being a danger to the public. He is unarmed and extremely happy. The authorities will most likely have him under control soon.*

As the cop chased him on the shoulder of the highway, Adnan saw there really was no realistic way out of the situation. The grassy area to the right merged upward into a hill which was quite high and then from the top it sharply descended into the picturesque town of Irving.

"Let's dance," said Adnan as he swerved right and went off the road. The hot rubber tires sizzled on the smooth, cool, velvet grass, sliding on it like a surfboard on water. The car, which had gained considerable speed and momentum on the highway, climbed the hill. The cop in pursuit slowed down and decided not to venture into this dangerous area. As the car sped up the hill to the top, Adnan was unable to slow it down; it was too late for that. Using the hill as a ramp, the car leaped into the sunny blue sky. The engine was still running but had no contribution to make, the tires were spinning but felt no road beneath them, and Adnan held the steering wheel. Even the goddess of gravity smiled at the brashness of this man gone wild. And on this beautiful sunny breezy day, she let him have a moment. Adnan looked downward and saw the city of Irving—neat and beautiful Irving with its restaurants and shops.

How many times he had met his manager and co-workers at the Chinese restaurant below to eat Mongolian beef and discuss when they should have the next meeting. Here he had fought with the sleep that comes from eating greasy food with plastic forks. He compared those meetings with the wild and present moment and decided he loved the now more than all the befores.

He landed on a quiet residential street, rattling every part of the car. The tires lost their hub caps. The air bag burst from the steering wheel and punched Adnan in the face. The car kept rolling and finally crashed into a dollar store. When he came out of shock, he was surrounded by cops. One officer handcuffed him while another held the large drink from which Adnan took some more sips. It was all caught on camera.

This was Adnan's first time in prison. He felt nervous, like a freshman in college who must learn to share limited living space with other wild men. But this was not college where roommates invent social networks and write blogs. He encountered for the first time people who were not from soft backgrounds. Men who did not own smart phones or laptops.

These men wore leather vests and bracelets. They had tattoos that had faded over time, earrings, teeth that had not seen a dentist, dried skin that made their knuckles look like small onions.

The largest among them, who was the leader because he wore a T-shirt that said *Boss,* was nearly seven feet tall. His head was shaved and his skin was a mixture of Europe, Africa, and Asia. It was as if the United Nations had selected him to represent every criminal on earth. He came and stood in front of Adnan who in his khakis, blue shirt, and brown leather shoes looked like a delicate flower in front of a rugged mountain of muscle and fat. This rough giant locked eyes with Adnan and asked, "Who the hell are you?"

Prison

"Do you like that?"

———————

"GOOD AFTERNOON," said Adnan. He used formal greetings to avoid conflict.

The giant moved closer to Adnan. "I thought I asked you a question. Who the hell are you?"

Adnan often borrowed audiobooks from the library, and when stuck in traffic jams he gained knowledge from recorded lectures given by professors of subjects like history, science, and ancient Egypt. Adnan attempted to combine all that knowledge in his answer.

"I suppose the answer to your question would be, I am a man. A biological being that has evolved over billions of years. In my skull I carry a brain—the most sophisticated thing in the entire universe. I am a collection of trillions of cells that are cooperating with one another to make my existence possible. I stare with wonder at the night sky and gazing at the stars I ask, *Is anyone out there?* So gentlemen, in closing I would like to say that I am a wonderful, curious being."

For a moment the rough men around him stood still. They had never heard such words. The criminal community avoids philosophical speculations because time is short and someone is always chasing them. But now a man stood among them offering the voice of reason. Scientific thoughts had arrived in a place of punishment.

They hit him.

And as they beat him they asked the confusing question: "Do you like that?"

After a few hits, they pushed him onto the floor and the giant sat on Adnan's stomach, grabbing Adnan's shirt collar to shake him. Adnan's stomach was providing seating comfort to this very large man who was hitting him. Adnan made a fist of his clean, moisturized fingers and with all his strength, he swung his fist at the jaw of this giant. The giant's chin felt like a wet suede shoe and the giant fell back, hitting his head against the wall.

Just then, a loud voice. "All right break it up, you animals. Are you causing trouble in here? Haven't you done enough on Highway 635?" It was the prison guard.

"Wait a second," said the giant as he rubbed his bruised chin. "You are the 635 bandit?"

"Yeah, he's the freak," said the policeman. "Now back off."

The giant was now smiling. Gone was the anger on his face. Suddenly he was a fan.

"Your driving was badass! You made it on *Hi There News*! They've been showing your driving footage all morning. When you drove through the dollar store you must have caused twenty-five dollars worth of damage."

The three rough men, who were only moments ago his enemies, now patted Adnan on the shoulder. For the first time, Adnan felt that he had found friends. Not "contacts" that you make on social-networking websites or people who live in your address book, but real friends who threaten you, choke you, and slapped you while kneeing your groin.

A beautiful and familiar voice distracted him from this networking session. "What has happened to you?"

It was Naureen. She could not believe her eyes. The simple, soft man she had known was now getting into fistfights in prison. She expressed her concerns. "Do you think you can just disappear for days? Do you have any sense of resp..."

34

Adnan placed his finger on her glossy lips. "Everything is good."

"But how? You suddenly left for Africa and I had to take care of everything at home, including dropping off and picking up the kids from school!"

"It was all worth it, Naureen," said Adnan.

"Why?"

"Because I quit my job."

"What?"

"I can do anything I want between the hours of nine and five."

"What will we do for money?"

"Money! Is that what worries you? There are higher things in life."

"Like what?"

"Like the blue sky. The white clouds that float in it, the golden sun that shines upon us now." The man had spoken from the heart, describing things we see daily yet don't appreciate.

Naureen felt the impact of these great words. Slowly she moved her hand through the iron bars that separated them and slapped his face.

"Wake up! The mortgage will be due in thirty days. We have credit-card debts and car payments. All the silly clouds and golden sunshine will not pay the bills!"

"Keep the clouds out of this, Naureen," said Adnan, defending nature. But she was right. And yet the euphoria of being a free man, not wanted in a boring office at nine a.m. continued to delight him even in prison.

The police officer was back. "All right time's up. Visiting time is over."

Naureen looked into his eyes. She saw a sparkle she had never seen. It was like a small star burning brightly. She failed to understand his joy under such circumstances and left without saying goodbye.

The giant came up to Adnan and patted him on the back. "Don't worry 635. We will figure out a way to pay your bills."

"How?"

"When we get out, we are planning to visit a bank."

"Oh, you have a checking account?"

"Let's just say we will be making a withdrawal, and we need a driver."

"Why don't you take the bus?"

"Let's just say that once we make the withdrawal we will need to leave quicker than we arrived. If you catch my drift."

"Why not call a cab? They are really quick."

"Let's just say that the police will be looking for us, and the cab driver might refuse to drive us."

"Why would the police be looking for you?"

"Because we'll rob the bank, you idiot!"

This is when Adnan understood the tragedy of prison and punishment. Men came here not to reflect on their mistakes or to plan a better life. They came here to become worse. The problem with man is that he wants a better life but without bettering himself. Adnan turned away from these men and turned on the television.

Welcome to Hi There News! We are interviewing Senator Neverist. He is an opponent of the marriage laws as applied to the Desis.

Reporter: Senator, welcome to our show.

Senator Neverist: It's good to be here.

Reporter: Senator, you are the greatest opponent of the Desi marriage laws. Now for our audience, we just want to clarify that the Desi Marriage Bill was signed into law by the president.

Senator: Yes, that was a tragic day.

Reporter: We want to quickly remind our audiences that the Desi marriage laws permit Desis to marry according to their own customs anywhere in the United States. That means that on the street, a Desi may drill holes into the road, hammer a large nail, and put up a tent to prepare for the happy occasion. Delightful ceremonies involving horses, elephants, and sometimes kangaroos are used at these events.

At Desi weddings, the groom usually arrives on a horse, accompanied by the magnificent beating of drums at midnight. To the sound of trumpets the bride arrives, sitting gracefully on an elephant, her eyes lowered in modesty.

Senator Neverist: How disruptive! People can't sleep at night because of these loud ceremonies.

Reporter: But Senator, Desis like to marry in places such as highways because of the smooth surface, and also at terminals at the airport or on the runways when no planes are landing.

Senator: Why should these immigrants have special rights? We need to strike down these laws, as they are un-American.

Reporter: But Senator, do we not have parades that disrupt traffic?

Senator: Yes, but those parades promote American culture.

Reporter: But Senator, the Desis have contributed billions to the economy, the catering businesses have made money, and the tent industry is absolutely delighted—they have expanded their business from camping to marriages.

Senator: Just think about the problems! Traffic was blocked on Highway 635 in Dallas when a Desi couple tied the knot under a large silk tent lighted by extravagant glowing oval-shaped lights. Then a bus was delayed in Nebraska because of an engagement ceremony where they carpeted an exit, using it to serve dinner. In Iowa an engagement celebration caused nine-hour delays due to synchronized dancing on the runway to express joy. Why do they get so excited? It's only an engagement!

Reporter: So what are you suggesting, Senator?

Senator: We must repeal these laws and banish Desi rituals in America. None of that synchronized dancing nonsense. No confusing dance-offs. No high-pitched singing.

Reporter: How do you intend to enforce this?

Senator: I have proposed that a new agency be formed to prevent any of these activities taking place—WTA, which stands for Watch Them Always. WTA will make sure that wherever an elephant or a horse is seen at a marriage ceremony, swift legal action is taken, and the bride and groom are arrested. And also the animals.

Reporter: But Senator, won't this cost the taxpayers money?
Senator: We must pay the price.

"What a jerk!" said the giant as he switched the television off.

"I will not let this happen," said Adnan.

"You planning to take him out?" asked the giant.

"You mean for dinner?"

"Do you plan to make him disappear?"

"I am going to write a letter," said Adnan. "Get me a paper and pencil."

"This is not a bookstore, 635."

And yet from his prison cell, in these trying circumstances, Adnan did find a paper and a gel-ink pen by asking for it. He wrote furiously, crossing out words and re-writing them till he had written his first letter to the world.

Destiny

"In America I changed many jobs because I wanted to diversify myself"

T THE time our great leader Adnan published
his famous letter from prison, I was working as a
marketing executive. My name is Minhaj. I was born
in Pakistan and grew up in the eighties. Pakistan had only one
government-controlled TV channel. This kept things simple.
We were one nation, under one God, watching one channel.
There was channel one and we were committed to watching
it. The divorce rate was low because no one was fighting for
the remote.

In the nineties, satellite TV arrived. Exciting shows on
different channels could now be seen. After watching a TV
show about glamorous people saving folks from drowning, I
decided that I wanted to come to America to become a life-
guard. I imagined myself running across the beach to save
lovely drowning girls. Sometimes I imagined saving three
girls at a time; they would be holding on to my two legs and
one hand, while I used the remaining hand to swim to shore
as people cheered for me. I discussed these aquatic desires
with my cousin, but he warned me.

"In America women wear miniskirts and people drink
alcohol till late hours of the night! Sometimes they go

bungee jumping. They live for this world and not the next. What will you do over there?" I went straight to the American embassy and applied for a visa. When my visa was approved I was thrilled. I was coming to America. The beach was waiting!

I landed in North Dakota.

Why North Dakota? Because I had an uncle living over there. And here's the thing you need to understand about Desis: we only go to places where a relative already resides. This is why Desis have never sent a man to the moon. It's not because we don't have the technology. It's because we don't have an uncle living up there.

In America I changed many jobs because I wanted to diversify myself. I delivered pizza, and I performed so well they promoted me to dishwasher. I also did some work for a famous supermarket but we ran into a disagreement—I wanted to work there and they wanted to fire me. On the same day they terminated me, I applied to a fast-food burger restaurant, but they kept rejecting my resume. When I followed up, they told me there were other applicants who were more qualified. How could that be? Did these applicants have a masters in deep frying or a PhD in french fries? On job applications I always wrote, "Not available for work on Wednesday, Thursdays and weekends."

One day I got a call from a deli shop that was well respected in sandwich circles. The manager sounded official on the phone.

"We would like to interview you for a marketing position."

I got really excited, re-brushed my teeth and got there. The manager met with me and presented me with a free sandwich. We talked about life and after hearing my views about the world he was so impressed that he made a decision right there. He did not feel the need to go home and discuss it with his wife. As a manager he sensed my quality.

"I want to offer you a marketing position with us."

"I want to thank you for that," I said trying to sound professional. Finally, a breakthrough! The manager was not done yet. I had made an excellent impression on him and he gave me some more good news.

"You will be the head of your department, and this job has a lot of flexibility."

"Your decision is most likable" I said as I tried to control my excitement.

"The uniform is a very important part of your job."

"I agree," I said and saluted him. I have always respected the uniform. Even on famous shows, all the lifeguards wore matching shirts and bathing suits. Throughout history women have wanted men in uniform because it represents a sense of purpose and fortitude. He handed me a colorful-looking packet of clothes. His eyes held great expectations.

"We want you to dress up as a clown and stand outside the store. And hold this sign up so that everyone can see it." It was a large sign that held these words in black and white: *Come on in and get a good meal for just $6.99!* He was right, it was a marketing position, but I wanted to be sure it was everything he said it would be.

"You did say that this job has a lot of flexibility," I asked.

"Oh yes," he said. "When you hold up the sign in your clown suit, I want you to dance and shake a little. That grabs their attention."

As the only clown there I was automatically the head of my department. The usual day began with me painting my face and placing a red ball on my nose. I would wear an orange wig and start dancing as soon as I reached my office, which was on the sidewalk outside the store.

It turned out that I was pretty good at the job. I realized that in life there are not that many professional opportunities available for a man to paint his face. There was a lot of job security and the lack of competition really helped me evolve as a clown. As a man who has no rhythm, I was free to dance without fear of criticism. No one could judge me. If I danced badly it was considered funny and therefore professional. I attracted a lot of attention, maintained physical fitness, and many customers came into the store for the six ninety-nine special.

One day the store manager called me into his office, which was behind the toaster oven. He praised me and offered me a promotion. "I'm making you manager of clowns. I want you to hire more clowns and grow the department."

Here I ran into problems. Clowns don't want to be managed—that's why they became clowns. They reject society. We never see a clown standing in line or filling out paper work or making a PowerPoint presentation. They walked out of all this. They had the last laugh. Besides, a lot of clowns I contacted were too proud. One clown after another said the same thing.

"I can juggle. I consider myself overqualified for this position."

In the clown community there is a hierarchy. If you can juggle three objects, you are considered a bachelor of fine arts. If you can ride a unicycle—those large one-wheel bikes—then you are considered a master of fine arts. By this time, most of these clowns are in so much demand they get hired by the circus, which is always hiring because of trampling incidents with the elephants. The circus is high prestige and cutting edge. Every clown wants the circus on his resume. And it is at the circus where most clowns complete their PhD by getting shot out of cannons.

For these reasons I never made it in the world of clown management. Still, I was doing well professionally. I had offers from other deli shops looking for clowns. And yet I could not help but feel that something even greater was calling me. Sure, I got free sandwiches and held balloons under the open sky, but was I really making a difference? I had come to America to be a part of something great. Maybe this was not it. It was with these doubts that I was eating lunch at an Indian restaurant when my eyes fell on a newspaper.

Hi There News

AN OPEN LETTER TO DESIS
by Adnan Raheem Khan

I write this letter from prison, where I am being held on traffic violation charges. My crime? I expressed excitement by driving fast, endangering the public, speeding up a hill, and landing inside a dollar store. For this, I am in jail. But another man who threatens our way of life is free. Senator Neverist. He speaks daily against the Desis and now threatens to strike down our freedom. But that is just the political problem. We have many other problems that I have had time to think about.

On the family front, there are reports that a Desi teenager told her parents to "talk to the hand." Forbidden sarcastic phrases such as "whatever" and "like I care" are in common use by members of our great nation. Parting words such as "may I take your leave," have now been replaced by "let's bounce," leading to confusion and many injuries. The time has come for change. I, Adnan Raheem Khan, your leader, now call upon all Desis to become members of a political organization. We will be called the Desi League. After my fruitful time in prison, I will be interviewing applicants for the governing council of the Desi League.

*Please Note: Hired employees are to be paid in TYD currency.

Flight

"The problem was that the interview date was just twenty-four hours away"

ALL MY life I had always wanted to make speeches to beautiful women and grateful farmers who would cheer for me as I said something great. If the League accepted me I could be part of something meaningful. The problem was that the interview date was just twenty-four hours away. And my travel budget was fifteen dollars. None of the airlines were offering tickets to Dallas for that price. They wanted at least $400. I turned to the Internet and found:

www.GodDamnCheapTickets.com

Here on this website were prices I could afford. I found a plane ticket to Dallas, Texas for just ten dollars. That included tax. The airline offering the ticket fare made this statement:

Hang-On Airlines, we try and fly together.

Departure from Love It & Leave It Airport: 12 Noon

Arrival at Dallas Hope So Airport: 5 p.m.

*Friendly Warning: Travel by air can be extremely dangerous, so anything is possible.

Next morning I arrived for my departure at Love It & Leave It Airport of North Dakota. This was a grassy ground with a runway in the middle. There was no building or control tower. A large mustard-colored plane stood on the runway. It reminded me of a loving grandmother who means well and cooks tasty things but perhaps should avoid driving on the highway.

The steps leading up to the door of the plane were made with so much care that each of them had the words "Watch your step" printed above them. They really cared about us customers and I liked that. A flight attendant who stood next to the staircase was so classy. On her neck was a white silk scarf with black polka dots. Her shiny hair was twisted into an elegant bun upon which she wore a small maroon hat with a white feather. Her blue blazer, crisp white blouse, and the black knee length skirt made me glad that I had worn a tuxedo. My mother had always told me to dress well when traveling. "You just get treated better."

The flight attendant held in her manicured fingers a loudspeaker into which she spoke. "Boarding will now begin for first-class passengers."

Right next to the flight attendant was a live band playing soft music to soothe the ears of the first-class passengers as they climbed up the stairs. Among these first-class passengers was a famous film star who starred in many exciting movies.

In his science fiction films, we learned about aliens. All aliens were into dissection. When they met humans, the aliens did not say hello or discuss the weather. It was always straight to the dissection table. All aliens were dedicated medical students from outer space and there was no small talk in them. In other films he showed us the power of sofas. Even if evil men with shaved heads fired machine guns at him, if he somehow managed to dive behind a sofa you just knew he was going to be okay. While the whole room was shredded, he always remained safe behind the sofa. Perhaps bullets felt shy when approaching the sofa and went elsewhere.

The famous film star, along with other first-class passengers ascended the stairs at a leisurely pace. Some were dressed in purple gowns, others in silk track suits, all looking fresh and happy, their lives supported by wealth inherited from some hardworking ancestor. The flight attendant followed them up the stairs and when all of them had entered, she stood inside the plane with the door open and made her second announcement.

"Boarding will now begin for middle class passengers."

At this announcement *Hang-On Airlines* ground crew came running forward and rolled away the staircase that had allowed the passengers to board the plane.

"Why are they removing the staircase?" I asked.

"Just watch," said the man next to me.

The ground crew returned with a large plank of wood, which they lifted and leaned against the door of the plane. The sheep that had been grazing nearby now climbed up this plank of wood and into the plane.

"Why are the animals boarding before us?"

"They paid more," he said.

"But they are animals!" I shouted.

"And you, sir, are a racist."

Once all the sheep had boarded the plane, the door to the plane was shut. We could see the heads of sheep through the windows as they sat comfortably in the back rows of the plane, and they were looking down on us. Then without warning the plane was moving on the runway.

"They are leaving without us!" I shouted.

"Wait for it," said the man next to me.

"But the plane is moving!"

"Wait for it," he kept saying like an idiot as the plane gathered speed on the runway. And then we saw the beautiful head of the flight attendant as she gracefully leaned out of a window and spoke to us using a loudspeaker.

"Economy passengers may now board the plane."

"How do we board the plane when it is moving and the plane door is shut!" I shouted.

"Wait for it," he kept blabbering away. I wanted to smack him.

And then I saw what he wanted me to wait for. Ropes. Ropes were being lowered from small holes in the plane. I saw that the only ones remaining were the economy passengers. Economy passengers were decent people like me—normal folks who buy things on sale, people who join fitness clubs and then can't get rid of the membership because they still live within a fifty-mile radius. Folks who went to college, work hard, and now eat at the finest fast-food restaurants and buy lottery tickets. We all ran toward the plane as it gathered speed on the runway.

The economy-class passengers ran like trained athletes, bags slung around their chests, attempting to catch the ropes. And then it hit me. That's what *Hang-On Airlines* was. You had to hang on! Clouds had gathered and decided to send rain upon us. As I ran on the wet runway I saw soft lighting inside the plane. The first-class passengers sipped wine and cuddled in soft blankets while a smiling flight attendant brought them piping-hot tasty foods, which they ate with the aid of toothpicks. They were also exchanging large amounts of cash with the flight attendant and pointing toward us. They were placing bets on who among us would catch the ropes and successfully board the plane. In their soft turtleneck sweaters with wine glasses in hand, they cheered for us as we slipped and ran desperately toward the ropes that they had hung for us. The sheep also watched from their cabin, bleating with encouragement. Or perhaps they were mocking us. I couldn't tell; it was all happening very quickly.

All of us who were running to grab the ropes hated one another. The other economy passengers sprinting on the runway were, after all, enemies. There were not enough ropes for all of us. The rain had made the ropes slippery, and some who tried to catch a rope slipped and fell hard on the concrete, feeling the agony at an emotional and physical level. As the defeated lay on the runway watching *Hang-On Airlines* get away, they shouted in pain, "Refund, Refund!"

Though their situation was tragic, we simply hopped over them like horses and kept running toward the plane, never losing the focus. Running besides me was a large bald man in a tweed jacket. But his face betrayed a softness that comes from staying indoors and doing paper work. I knew I could take him down.

He looked at me and shouted. "Oh look! I can't believe it! It's a fairy!" It was a stressful time and the supernatural seemed possible. I turned around to look. There was nothing. No fairy. Not even a decent goblin. He had lied. Using this moment of distraction he pushed me aside and grabbed the last rope available. The rope that I had almost reached. How could I fall for this? I ran faster determined to catch the next rope but the plane was getting away. My anger at this man who had deceived me turned into animal energy, and I dived like an angry panther and caught his egs.

"What are you doing! You'll kill both of us," he shouted.

I could barely hear him as the plane was gathering speed for take off. I held on to his leg and even debated biting it to teach him a lesson. But then I decided against it for obvious reasons.

"Why did you deceive me with the fairy?" I shouted.

"I actually don't know why I did it," he said. "I am a decent man but competitive travel brings out the worst in me. I'm a librarian. I work in the kids' section. I do story time!"

"That explains the fairy," I said.

"I am a good person!"

"If that is true then redeem yourself as a good man and use your legs to pull me up!"

"I don't know if I can do this," he said. "I am a librarian who became a barbarian!"

The plane had taken off and the buildings of North Dakota appeared as a toy land.

"This is not the time to feel guilty," I said. "I know that competitive travel has drained you of all moral energy. But in this evil you are not alone. Even on the roads every day very nice people become raving mad when driving in traffic. It's not you, it's the system."

"But what about individual responsibility? We can't blame society for our actions."

"Sometimes society is wrong. If many good people tend to behave badly then we have to say that the environment they are placed in must have something to do with it. Think about it. In the library, which is a wonderful place, you do great things for kids and all visitors. But today, due to a high pressure moment, you became an animal. It's the environment, not you."

"Thanks for saying that. I do feel better now."

I had forgiven him because I have a large heart and also because I did not want to die. We were now in the sky and the wind wanted to separate me from his leg. The librarian with a shout that gave him strength, pulled himself up just enough to give me access to the same rope he was using. I grabbed the rope with both hands. The Economy passengers who had already made it to the top of the plane were safe. The roof of the plane had hooks to which these passengers had tied themselves with the ropes. They now pulled us up and we made it to the roof! Everyone on top of the plane had been listening to our conversation and they clapped for us.

"We did it!" I shouted. The librarian, who only minutes before had deceived me with a fairy tale, now shook my hand as if I was his brother. All was forgotten. The plane had ascended above the clouds of rain. We were again surrounded by the bright blue sky and *Hang-On Airlines* sailed on an ocean of clouds. On the loud speaker we heard this announcement.

Welcome to Hang-On Airlines. First class and middle class passengers may now unlock their seat belts. Economy passengers are advised to hang on to prevent injuries and probable death. We will be arriving in Dallas, Texas in five hours.

"Here is a man who, sees behind the scenes"

—————

AFTER HANGING on for many hours we landed at the Dallas Hope So Airport. I got a cab and immediately liked this land of leather boots and cowboys. Dallas, an elegant sun-soaked city with well-maintained roads, had on its state flag one large star. This I took as a good sign. Perhaps here I could reach stardom. I took a cab from the airport to Adnan's house.

I was surprised to see that his house was very normal and gave no hint of his high status among the leaders of the world. I knocked on the door and it was answered by Adnan himself. He was wearing a dark-blue suit with a dull-green tie and his hair was neatly parted from the side.

He greeted me pleasantly. "Yes?"

"My name is Minhaj and I am here for the interview."

"We have hired everyone already. But thank you for coming. May I offer you an orange drink?"

"Sir," I said, attempting to control my sadness, "after reading your letter in *Hi There News*, I knew my destiny. I literally grabbed the last available place on the flight. I am not leaving without an interview. And yes, I will have some tasty, ice-cold orange soda."

"When I wrote that letter from prison I was a little over-excited. I hope you have other options. Due to budget reasons, this job pays in TYD currency."

"What is that?"

"Thank You Dollars," he said. "Due to my current unemployed status, I pay people with gratitude."

I could not believe it! This man was a genius! Soon we were in the kitchen drinking tasty, cold orange soda. There another miracle happened. His wife, Naureen, the First Lady, walked into the kitchen with a frown on her face. It was apparent that she was not very happy with Adnan. She looked familiar and then it hit me! I had seen her dancing at a wedding celebration in Karachi many years ago.

"Were you at Zooby's wedding?" I asked.

"Yes. How do you know Zooby?"

"Zooby is my second cousin's first cousin," I said, almost shouting with joy.

"Oh, Zooby is my cousin too!"

I was standing with family. Though this was a pleasant surprise, it is not shocking. Every Desi has at least five hundred cousins. So the chances of being related are high. There is even a legend where an evil man kidnapped a child and called up the parents to demand a ransom. The parents of the boy convinced the kidnapper that he was their cousin. The little boy also relaxed knowing that he was with his uncle. Finally the demand for ransom turned into a family reunion and no one had to die. This is how strong the cousin network is among Desis. It can save lives. And now it would change mine.

Naureen smiled at the memory of Zooby's wedding but did not make eye contact with Adnan, who was attempting to join the conversation.

"But why have you come here? You must be studying. Why do you want to be a part of his madness? Even though he is my husband," she said pointing to her head, "he is not completely okay in here."

"Oh no! I read his letter in *Hi There News*! Your husband is a great man. He is standing up for the Desis in America."

Naureen was not too convinced, but talking about Pakistan cheered her up. It seemed that though she lived in America physically, mentally, spiritually, and food-ually she was in Karachi.

I spent the next hour discussing all the new restaurants that had opened in Karachi. Naureen laughed a lot while ironing her clothes using spray starch at appropriate intervals. Her son Bubloo was a chubby, excitable boy of eleven. We played "Name, Place, Animal, Thing," a game involving naming things that begin with a certain letter of the alphabet. He cheated. Finally Adnan came in the living room and invited me to the interview.

"Minhaj! The league is now in session. You may enter for your interview."

I walked into his office, and Adnan pulled the shower curtain shut. Adnan introduced me to the two other men in this room.

"This is Mr. Maaf Karna. He has a PhD in international relations." Mr. Maaf Karna was a chubby man in his forties with a thin mustache and thick hair, which he kept neatly combed with the use of oil. He smiled only for a second, stretching his lips to barely meet the requirements of civilized behavior. Why even smile if you are going to do it like that? I was so impressed by the introduction that it made me even more nervous. My voice shook as I greeted Mr. Maaf Karna. Then Adnan introduced me to the other man. He was a small, angry-looking man with thick graying hair. Also in his forties. He wore glasses and had several ball point pens in the pocket of his short-sleeve shirt.

"This is Mr. Hisaab Khan. He has a master's in mathematics and is the author of *Mathematical Reasons to Love Math*."

I, of course, have hated math since my childhood, and I was very easily able to transfer those very feelings toward this man. To me he represented fractions, which had been my childhood enemy. He did not shake my hand, and I took the third chair at the desk. We sat facing Adnan, who smiled politely. Mr. Maaf Karna was in a hurry to begin the interview and cleared his throat in a manner that signaled his impatience. Both he and Hisaab Khan tilted their chairs in my direction and stared at me, which made me sweat with anxiety. While I love judging others and even watch shows that allow me to text my judgment, I hate it when it is done to me.

Mr. Maaf Karna began the interview as he scanned my resume while scratching his chin. "Forgive me, but I have been looking at your curriculum vitae, and it doesn't look very good."

"My what?" "Your curriculum vitae."

I felt this was some kind of a disease and I wanted to remove any misunderstanding. "I don't have that, sir. I am perfectly healthy."

"Forgive me, but everyone has it!" he said.

"I don't have it, sir." And I felt grateful.

At my saying this, Hisaab Khan grabbed the paper from Maaf Karna's hand and waved it in the air like an angry school teacher. "What am I holding in my hand right now?"

"Paper," I said.

"Your resume," said Hisaab Khan with a grunt. "curriculum vitae is Latin for resume."

"Is Latin a requirement for this job?" I asked.

"No, it is not," said Adnan. "I don't see us talking to the Vatican anytime soon."

Hisaab Khan shook his head, and Maaf Karna exhaled sharply to express his disappointment in carbon dioxide.

Maaf Karna summarized his opinion of my existence based on the resume I had given them. "Forgive me for saying this, but your resume is not professional. There are spelling mistakes. More than half of the resume is the hobby section, which includes irrelevant information such as cutting out with great precision the magazine pictures of famous film actresses, and eating doughnuts slowly. You also write in capital letters that you love sword fighting."

"Not as a participant, though," I clarified, "because that is stressful. But when others do it for the sake of honor, I admire them."

"Again irrelevant," said Maaf Karna. "We will not require any of your hobbies or likes and dislikes. And you spelled resume wrong."

"I made the resume on the flight. There was a lot of movement so it's not perfect."

Maaf Karna was not convinced and continued his assault on my humanity. "Under education you write that you are a permanent student of Life University. Forgive me for asking, but what does that mean?"

"I believe that life is the best teacher. I am a student of life," I said with a confident smile.

"But is that a certified institution recognized by the Department of Education?"

"I love Life University because we are automatically enrolled the day we are born. There are no requirements to get in. If you are breathing, you are in!"

Finally Adnan injected some positivity into the interview. "Well spoken!"

But neither Hisaab Khan nor Maaf Karna was happy with Life University. They wanted it to be recognized by some institution. I could tell they were into paper work.

Maaf Karna continued in his special manner. "Forgive me, but you..."

"I forgive you," I said. He had been seeking forgiveness since the beginning of the interview. I felt I had to forgive him.

"That's not what I meant!" he said angrily.

Then Adnan asked a question. "You write in your resume that you have experience in marketing. Would you like to tell us a little bit about that?"

"Yes. My job involves attracting customers. I try to get their attention and if all goes well, they purchase our product."

"Could you be more specific?"

"I am a clown, dancing for the company that hired me."

For some reason this resonated with Adnan and he heartily approved of my job description. "Aren't we all! Young man, that is poetic! Aren't we all! Clowns, gentlemen, we are all clowns in this circus of life. Here is a man who sees behind the scenes."

This gave me some confidence and I got more comfortable. But Maaf Karna was still upset about me forgiving him. He remained silent and serious.

Hisaab Khan, who was looking at me through his glasses, spoke to me with some anger. "I am going to ask you mathematical questions."

I hate math. A subject so troublesome that even the questions are called problems. But there was no escaping it.

Hisaab Khan almost barked the first question. "What is the value of pie?"

"Well, it depends," I said.

"On what?"

"On how hungry you are."

"No!" said Hisaab Khan. A word he seemed to enjoy using. "It is 3.14." He sounded so sure about it! I did not want to argue with this man even though I had eaten pie for ninety-nine cents. There was in his eyes a certain sense of superiority that comes from number crunching and an anger on his face that comes from never having a girlfriend. He continued with his questions that now focused on the one thing that I hated most. Fractions.

"Let me give you a situation. It is Jennifer's birthday. Her mother has baked her a cake."

"Is it chocolate?"

"That is not important. Now every guest is supposed to get one piece of cake. Two-fifths of the cake is eaten. What fraction of the cake must Jennifer cut for the five remaining guests so that her uncle can also enjoy cake when he arrives late at the party?"

"Why is the uncle late?"

"That is not important," said Hisaab Khan, smiling; but it was an offensive smile. "Just tell me how to solve this problem."

"Oh that's easy," I said. "Just go down to the grocery store and get more cake. That's my American solution. Food is so cheap here! Everyone wins and her uncle can eat all the cake he wants."

"That is not the answer. You are wrong!"

"I don't know. If I were the uncle, I would love to have a whole cake waiting for me. It's nice to have more when you are eating cake, especially if you have been traveling."

"Wrong, wrong, wrong!" Hisaab Khan was turning red.

I remained silent. Then it was Maaf Karna's turn.

"You write on your resume that your typing speed is above 300. Forgive me but that sounds like a world record."

"Yes, I do type very fast."

"You do? Forgive me, but you are absolutely sure about that?" His voice was rising in anger and yet he was also asking forgiveness.

"Yes," I said. "But not in word format."

"What do you mean?"

"The letters that I type, they do not form words."

"Forgive me, but what do they form?"

The interview, I felt, was not going as well as I had expected.

Question of Leadership

"They see these thrilling things and they desire to take it all home"

—————

"THE DESI League intends to solve the problems of our community by creative thinking," said Adnan. "Can you describe a situation at work where you took ownership of a project? What problems did you face and how did you try to resolve them?"

Even before I could answer, Maaf Karna added his own comment. "Forgive me, but I doubt he has any such experience."

"I used to work at a supermarket," I said quickly, to take away the attention from Maaf Karna. "I love that store! It's amazing because it allows us to buy all the things that China has to offer. But there is one thing that still bothers me about that place."

Adnan was intrigued. "What?"

"Florescent lights," I said. "They have too many of them. Fluorescent lighting makes everything ugly. The furniture looks basic. Even liquid soap loses its beauty."

"What does all this have to do with the question we asked you?" asked Hisaab Khan.

"In this lighting it is impossible to sell products properly. Especially scented candles. I felt they were not presented properly."

"Can you explain that?" asked Adnan.

"We had all these beautiful scented candles but their true beauty and function could not be appreciated. For example, if you go to the electronics section, the flat screen TVs are playing famous movies. Customers go over there, they see with their eyes superheroes saving women dangling from bridges, cop cars chasing evil men. They see these thrilling things and they desire to take it all home."

"Yes," said Adnan. "I am always attracted to the TV section."

"Exactly!" I said, feeling happy that Adnan was agreeing with me. "I felt that the scented-candle section did not have this excitement. These givers of light and joy sat silently on boring metallic shelves. So I took the lead. One Sunday afternoon, when everyone and their cousin comes to the supermarket, I decided to take independent action."

Even Maaf Karna was now hooked. "Forgive me, but what did you do?"

"I went to the main electrical room and I switched off the main power. The whole store fell into darkness. I used a lighter to light the scented candles. I lit the butternut, and the fragrance of butter filled the store. I lit the apple-seed candle and fresh apples came to life. Each candle became a glowing lighthouse attracting everyone to its beauty in a place that had once been tortured by fluorescent lighting."

"But how did the people react to the darkness?" asked Adnan.

"There was screaming. Trolleys got mixed up and I think three people were arrested because they got into a fight. One man stole a cycle by cycling out of the store. Some children got exchanged but later they were reunited with their real parents on a talk show. The police arrived soon and turned on the ugly lighting. The management who had seen me lighting the candles applauded my "reacting to an emergency." But when I told them that it was I who had turned the main switch off, they got very upset and told me to leave and never come back."

"Forgive me for saying this, but that's exactly what I want to tell you."

I ignored Mr. Maaf Karna. "So what did I learn from this leadership experience? People are not always going to appreciate my contributions. I just have to believe in myself and keep trying."

My story had made such a huge impact that they were all staring at me with their eyes wide open. I had made such an impression that it took some time for Adnan to speak again.

"Describe for us a situation in which you had to work with a really challenging problem. How did you handle this? Is there anything you would have done differently in hindsight?"

"When I was delivering pizza, I got out of the car at the address. There was a grassy area in front of the house. I was already competing with my enemies on who could deliver more pizzas that day."

"You had enemies?" asked Adnan.

"My co-workers," I replied.

Maaf Karna and Hisaab Khan looked at each other and shook their heads. Adnan asked me to continue.

"So as I get out of the car, I run towards the house with their pizza. They had just mowed their lawn and it had rained earlier. I was sprinting and I lost my balance. Unfortunately the pizza box was not closed properly and the pizza slipped out of the box and fell splat on the ground."

"Because you did not close it properly," said Hisaab Khan.

"Allow him to finish," said Adnan who was listening with great attention.

"What was worse? It was the cheesy side that hit the ground. The pizza became a magnet for pieces of grass on this freshly mowed lawn. When I picked up the pizza it was green with bits of grass. There was no way I could take the grass out.

Luckily for me the customers had ordered a veggie lovers. I knew from science that grass is a vegetable. But it stood out a little bit and looked too fresh compared to the black olives. Using my leadership skills I broke some leaves from a nearby bush and, using my training as a food service employee, I distributed these leaves equally all over the pizza. These leaves made the grass look more normal. I put the pizza back in to the box and delivered it."

"Forgive me, but that kind of behavior is criminal," said Mr. Maaf Karna.

"So two good things came out of this," I said. "I never had to go back and get a new pizza and the customers got two extra toppings."

Adnan quickly moved to the last question. "What are your long-range goals and objectives for the next five to seven years? What would you find most rewarding about working with us?"

"I would like to have a private jet. Wear a three-piece suit. I love to travel. So if there are any meetings or conferences that you want me to attend—in Switzerland for example—I would like that. I would also like to have a secretary. She needs to be loyal and lethal in the use of kung fu but gentle in manner and voice. Someone who will defend and die for me even if I were to be attacked by lions. I guess she should have long hair and a beautiful smile."

Maaf Karna looked upset and he spoke to Adnan. "Forgive me, sir, but this man is not suitable for our organization or even for society in general."

Hisaab Khan agreed as well. "He does not know the value of pi, he has no respect for numbers, he obviously can't type, and he has been fired for playing with fire. The numbers just don't add up for him."

Adnan looked at the ceiling. His arms were folded across his chest. The great man was thinking. And then he spoke to give his decision. "Minhaj I want to thank you for coming to this interview. But I am afraid that we can't …"

Just then the shower curtain to his office was pushed aside by a delicate hand. It was Naureen and she spoke only to me.

"Minhaj, don't leave without dinner. I have cooked biryani and thinly sliced potato chips."

"Thank you!" I said. I love biryani with all my heart and it goes really well with fried potato chips because they add the crunch to it. Adnan was even happier. When Naureen left, he addressed the members of the league in his official presidential manner.

"Gentlemen, my wife has not made biryani in fourteen months. Minhaj made it happen. As president of the Desi League, I now confirm him as a member of the governing council. Minhaj, welcome to our team. Our mission is simple."

"And what is that, sir?" I asked, my voice shaking with excitement.

"Change the world."

"This man scores zero on the interview!" said Hisaab Khan. He even made a zero with his fingers and shouted, "Zero!"

Mr. Maaf Karna was also very angry. "Forgive me for saying this, but…"

At him saying this, I could not control myself any longer. I leaped from my chair and placed both my hands on his face using my palms to make a face sandwich. Looking into his eyes I said with joy, "I forgive you, I forgive you!"

"That's not what I meant," he shouted.

Weird.

Daily Responsibilities

"But at this they only laughed loudly"

S INCE ADNAN Raheem Khan was paying me in Thank You Dollars, I had requested free room and meals. I would occupy the couch in the living room. I resigned my job as a clown and took up this position as a full member of the Desi League.

I don't want to say nice things about myself because I think the correct procedure is to wait for others to give a compliment and then experience happiness…and yet I must say that I was the driving force behind the Desi League. I drove the children to school, I drove Adnan's mother to the mall, where the great woman updated herself on what the latest comforters looked like. Adnan's mother held two great distinctions. She was the mother of Adnan, which is a great honor. But she was also known as the *"Mother of All Coupons"* and obtained a discount at every store.

Since Adnan's license was suspended, I also drove him to a bookstore each evening. It was a large and beautiful bookstore that he referred to as the temple. While he browsed the history section I spent most of my time in the coffee area. I never drank the coffee. I ate the tasty carrot cakes, slices of chocolate-covered cheesecake, and many pretzels stuffed with spinach and cheese. Sometimes I went with the asiago cheese bagel. It is filled with cheese and when toasted, the cheese melts slightly, making it tasty as well as aromatic. The coffee section was proud that they offered paninis. Everyone loved asking, "Can I have a panini please?" No one used the word sandwich because the world had grown tired of it and the panini had taken over.

Most interactions went like this: "What kind of panini would you like, sir?'

"What paninis do you have, ma'am?"

"Oh, we have the chicken panini, the cheese panini..."

Sitting with my tomato and cheese panini I would study magazines, updating myself on who was having whose baby and who had lost too much weight and when everyone was coming out of rehab.

After reading biographies and books on history, Adnan would be done for the day. On the way back in the car, he would speak enthusiastically about the great men he had read about. Even when I played the radio very loudly, he would keep going. I think his mind was so filled with thoughts and ideas that he wished to live them in his life. He wanted to discuss Socrates and Plato at the dinner table. But his mother would inform him about the latest discounts available at the mall and Naureen had only one question.

"Did Socrates have a job?"

Adnan, being a family man, wanted to improve the "home climate" and decided to cheer up Naureen. This became clear to me when Adnan offered to go with Naureen to a furniture store. It was an interesting European store that sold affordable furniture in the form of jigsaw puzzles. Adnan was attempting to "win her back," as he had told me in his office. "Behind every great man," he said with a thoughtful look, "there is a woman who does not strangle him while he is sleeping." Before they went to the furniture store, they made the most difficult request.

"We'll be back in a few hours. Can you please make sure that the kids go to sleep on time?"

This was a huge responsibility. I had never put the kids to bed. Adnan's mother had gone to Houston to visit relatives. It was just me. Was I to sing them songs as they fell into dreamland? Was I to examine their tiny teeth to be sure they had flossed? Bubloo and Tina were not very well behaved. They misused their energies and both brother and sister had declared war on furniture. Tina, at the age of thirteen, considered herself an artist. Often she would put a chair on the table, and then on the chair she would put a stool and upon this stool a lamp. She called it a "*domestic pyramid*" and considered herself to be different and much more intelligent than kids her own age. Then there was Bubloo. He liked to jump over things. Like most Desi kids he was convinced that he was running the hundred-meter hurdle inside the living room. Even at the age of nine, Bubloo had not completely grasped gravity and considered it his 'best friend.' When I tried to explain to him that gravity was a force to be respected and even feared, he said, "No, I like to play with him."

As soon as Adnan and his wife left, the trouble began. Bubloo was jumping on the sofa and Tina decided to make a domestic pyramid in the living room. Finally, when I got them to the room that they shared, they continued their antics, with Bubloo doing somersaults on the bed. Using it like a trampoline he performed stunts, sometimes landing on his back sometimes falling on his front. It was only natural that children of this day and age should be like that. They admired vampires, they played video games on very small handheld devices. This had made them unstable. I warned them again and again that if they did not go to sleep then Bhudda Baba would show up. Bhudda Baba or Scary Old Man is what Desis use to terrify children into obedience.

But at this they only laughed loudly. "We are kids of the twenty-first century. We know there is no such thing as Bhudda Baba. Or job security."

In frustration, I called Adnan on his cell phone. He was in the kitchen section of the store and making a great show of interest in the color of cabinets.

"Hey Minhaj how is it going?"

"The children are behaving like wild animals. They are not listening to me."

"Listen Minhaj, this is my chance to make Naureen a little happy after that driving incident on the highway. And my going to Africa made her very angry. But I am getting her back. The kitchen cabinet section is saving my marriage."

"I understand sir, but what should I do with Bubloo & Tina?"

"Did you try Bhudda Baba?"

"Oh yes. I tried to scare them, but they laughed at me."

"Okay. Just call Bhudda Baba then. I'll give you his number."

"But I thought Bhudda Baba was just a mythological creation to scare children."

"No, he is real. My mother gave me this coupon for a special day and I guess we need to use it now." Adnan gave me an 800 number for Bhudda Baba and also a coupon code for discount.

I immediately called the number and heard this message:

- For Santa Claus, press one
- For God, press two
- To resolve world hunger, press three
- To bring back people from the dead, press four
- To end all wars, press five
- To page Bhudda Baba, press six
- To repeat all these options, press nine

Though I was intrigued by all these great options, I decided to press six for Bhudda Baba. When I pressed the number six, an electronic message announced, *"Please hang up or dial again."*

I put the phone down and went back to the kids' room. Bubloo was now doing a handstand on the edge of his bed and Tina's domestic pyramid had coffee mugs, a china vase, and a laptop. They were both wide awake and showed no signs of sleepiness.

"I have called Bhudda Baba and he will be here soon," I said, hoping that they would fall for it. But they continued their shouting and silliness.

Just then a large booming voice, as if from the heavens, thundered, *"I am Bhudda Baba!"*

The children screamed in terror. Even I got scared. It was an unnatural voice, too loud to be human.

"Turn the lights off," the great voice commanded. I ran to the switch and turned the lights off. The children had already crawled into bed and were shivering with fear. And then the door to the room opened slowly. Creaking. In the darkness we could make out a tall figure about seven feet high, in a robe.

"It's him," shouted Bubloo.

"It's Bhudda Baba! He actually does exist," cried Tina.

And then a small bluish light emerged from his very being. Was this a spirit or demon? We could only wonder in fear.

"What the hell is that light?" cried Bubloo in his trembling voice.

"It's my cell phone. Now fall asleep!" The booming voice echoed all over the house and perhaps up to the heavens.

"Please forgive us for his language," cried Tina. "He gets it from late night television."

"Language is not my department. Just go to sleep and don't ever stay awake late again. Do you hear me?"

"Yes, Bhudda Baba, we hear you loud and clear. We will sleep now. Thanks again for reminding us," said Tina, who had ignored all my requests only minutes ago. These kids who had mocked me all evening had become polite! They shut their eyes tightly and fell asleep.

"Wow," I said. "You are good."

"I'm a professional," he said in a normal voice. It was no longer booming or loud.

"Is there a restroom around here? I'd like to freshen up. I need to hit a few homes tonight."

When he came back his hair was gelled back. I was standing in the presence of legend.

"Your name is known to millions of people all over the world. I always thought of you as someone out of an ancient fairy tale. But you are quite modern. You have a cell phone. How did you start doing this?"

"It's a family tradition," he said.

"How did it begin?"

"Long time ago there was a young prince who did not like to go to bed early."

"Because he wanted to watch television?"

"There was no television back then. I am talking about a thousand years ago. So his mother the queen came up with a plan. She ordered one of her tallest servants to wear a long black robe."

"To scare the young prince?"

"Well he wasn't supposed to be scary. Bhudda Baba was originally a storyteller. But over time he was changed into someone scary."

"Why?"

"Parents wanted quick results. When these children grew up and had disobedient children of their own, they realized they needed Bhudda Baba. So they resorted to fear. They selected an even taller man. With his flowing robe, to the children it appeared as if this man was floating instead of walking.

72

Whenever the children did not sleep on time, Bhudda Baba was summoned."

"That must have scared them!" I said.

"Yes, but Bhudda Baba got a lot of things done. Homework, exercise, obedience. But over the years as monarchies declined, Bhudda Baba had to seek work elsewhere. So what was once a glorious royal tradition became a lousy night shift. Shopkeepers, teachers, and politicians were the new clients. They paid less and demanded more. No class. Anyway, the job was passed from son to son and I am now the living Bhudda Baba. But keep these words I tell you a secret. Especially from the kids. Children obey mystery."

He revealed the source of his loudness by showing me the speakers attached to his belt.

"They can go concert loud, if needed."

"Your robe is very impressive," I said.

"It is the original, given by the queen to my great ancestor the first Bhudda Baba. Touch it. Go on, feel the fabric."

I touched a thousand years of history. Once given by a queen to a slave, it was surprisingly soft for something feared. It had many patches, no doubt created over hundreds of years, to hold this historical garment together. The children were asleep and I watched him leave, his dark robe fading into the night.

Presidential Decision

"I have existed too long without inspiration"

WHILE RELATIONS were improving between Adnan and Naureen, relations between the Desis and the rest of America were deteriorating. Senator Neverist continued to criticize the Desi way of life and especially the marriage rituals that had brought so much delight to our community, to the world, and to some of the couples who had gotten married.

The Senator's campaign had turned the people against the Desis. At a wedding gathering held at the runway of an airport, Desis were booed for erecting a tent and dancing. Some drivers expressed rage by honking when Desis blocked exits, carpeted them with thick Persian rugs, and held an engagement dinner. Hate mail arrived at Desi homes delivered by a postman who also hated them but continued to deliver the mail because it was hateful.

Adnan called an emergency meeting in his home office. The shower curtain was drawn shut and the red light bulb was switched on to symbolize the importance of this meeting. The whole Desi League high command was there. All four of us. Maaf, Hisaab, and I sat on chairs facing Adnan, who sat at his desk under the map of the world. On the desk were some

important items that allowed us to brainstorm: roasted peanuts, french fries, hot sauce, and cold cans of orange soda.

"America is turning against us," said Adnan, joining his
hands by intertwining his fingers, which allowed him to think
deeply on important matters.

"Forgive me for saying this," said Maaf Karna while crunching a peanut in his boring mouth, "but this will only get worse.
Senator Neverist is about to address the whole country at a
press conference in Washington, DC."

Hisaab Khan poured cold soda into a glass, probably
counting the bubbles in his sick mind.

"The Senator has made a calculation. He blames the Desis
and he gets popular."

"Forgive me," said Maaf Karna. "But we have meetings in
your home office, we turn on the red bulb, but do we really
make a difference? Politics is for rich men. In any case, it all
gets decided at the top."

If that was not negative enough, Hisaab Khan added his
own warning to Adnan. "You are an unemployed man with a
family and a mortgage. Should you even be thinking of these
political matters?"

"Yes, I should," said Adnan. "I am more than a worker
in need of survival. I am a man with feelings and ideas. Do
you know we have sixty thousand thoughts every day! Sixty
thousand, gentlemen! Yet we waste these thoughts on small
matters like bills and worries. I want to use this power for the
good of man."

"Forgive me, but why not use these thoughts to get a job?"

"I have existed too long without inspiration," said Adnan,
looking deeply into the shower curtain. Now I want to live.
It is said that if we silence the sounds of doubt, something
happens."

"Forgive me, but nothing will happen."

"Wise men, prophets, and fortune-tellers speak of a mental state. In this state we can do no wrong. I seek this."

"Forgive me for saying this, but you need to stop listening to self-help audiobooks and face reality. All this sounds like a lot of rubbish to me."

Adnan had heard enough. He stood up like a leader and made a presidential decision. "Gentlemen, my wife thinks I am going to Washington, DC, for an IT consulting contract. She is innocent because she does not know what I intend to do. I have decided to confront Senator Neverist at the Capitol."

"Forgive me, but why should we go all the way to Washington, DC? We can register our protest here in Texas by writing a strongly worded e-mail to our newspaper."

"Alexander the Great conquered the Persian empire by attacking the emperor's chariot. He did not waste time on strongly worded papyrus letters," said Adnan.

Maaf Karna was not convinced. "Forgive me, but you need to stop watching documentaries. It is driving you mad."

Adnan was already implementing his decision. "Due to budget constraints we will go by car."

The first vote was held. We devised a sophisticated manner of voting. A roasted peanut meant a yes vote and a popcorn represented a no. Adnan placed a peanut in the center of the desk. Hisaab Khan and Maaf Karna placed two defiant popcorns in front of Adnan's peanut. The three of them stared at me with hopes in their eyes. I promptly added a supportive roasted peanut, allying myself with Adnan. Adnan used his position as the president of the league and vetoed both of them. Democracy was victorious. We were going to Washington, DC.

"I was falling into an oil painting"

THANKS TO a coupon presented to the Desi League by Adnan's mother, we rented a gleaming purple convertible which could comfortably seat four fully grown men.

On this trip Adnan promoted me to COS (Chief of Snacks). I provided the league members with supplies of chocolate covered almonds, and different variations of potato chips. As we began our journey driving through the great land of Texas, Adnan developed a deep affection for kettle-cooked potato chips and crunched his way through a whole large bag in the very first hour of our journey.

Adnan had brought with him a number of music CDs. He had a habit of only listening to the first fifteen seconds of a song. After barely fifteen seconds he would skip to the next song.

"I am seeking inspiration," he explained to the rest of us, who were getting frustrated with his fidgeting. "I love this part, I love this part," he would say holding down the rewind button, listening to one line of a song again and again. Maaf Karna and Hisaab Khan did not love this, and when Adnan was purchasing a fish sandwich at a famous fast-food restaurant, they took out all his CDs and threw them in the trash.

I was the driver when we entered the state of Arkansas. Everyone had fallen asleep and I frankly enjoyed the break from their voices. It was raining. I love how rain falls on glass like a thin rope that shatters into a thousand diamonds. Out of respect for the beauty of nature, I did not turn on the wiper. I felt no need to wash away the beauty. Thick droplets of water absorbed all the color and light. The trees blurred into blobs of green, and lights from other cars became candy-colored rivers sliding down the windshield. All the colors merged together and I felt like I was falling into an oil painting. One more thing that was part of this gorgeous blurriness was the exit sign which I missed while having this magical experience. When the rain stopped falling I realized I was lost. I took the next exit which led me to a bumpy road. The shaking woke up the sleeping passengers.

"Where are we?" asked Adnan.

The road was not well lit, and large trees surrounded us. In the distance we saw a flickering light. As we drove closer it appeared to be a campfire. We decided to drive up to it and get help with directions. As our car made its way toward this camp, the road beneath the wheels became even rougher and we were climbing over stones and sticks. I stopped the car under a tree.

We were talking among ourselves when someone sharply knocked on my window. I turned to my left and saw in the darkness a man. The light from my dashboard revealed his twinkling eyes and large white teeth. And then we saw that he was not alone. Behind him were a number of men; some of them had surrounded our car. Where had we arrived?

"Our ancestors avoided dangerous animals by running"

I LOWERED THE window and Adnan leaned forward to speak to them.

"We have lost our way. Can you help us?"

"Everything happens for a reason," said the tallest among them who stood in front of the car. His voice was deep and commanding. "You are among the tribe of Missisoka. I am the leader."

"Forgive me for saying this," whispered Maaf Karna. "They look dangerous."

"They outnumber us," added Hisab Khan. "If we get out of the car they may do as they wish."

Our anxious discussion was interrupted by the leader's loud manly voice. "How far must you travel?"

"We are on our way to Washington, DC," said Adnan.

The leader came forward and opened the passenger door to let Adnan out. "You have many miles to go. You will spend the night here."

Even before anyone could object, Adnan got out of the car and shook hands with the leader. Maaf Karna and Hisaab Khan got out of the car grumbling, but they did it softly because they were scared of these large and robust men. In the darkness we all followed the leader and his men. He led us on a trail through the trees. We could barely see the man ahead of us, and walking with strangers in the dark seemed like a mistake. Just then the trees around us disappeared. The night sky was once again visible with stars and a full moon that turned the grass luminous blue. We stood on the edge of a large field. In the distance, in the center of this field, was a large fire.

The flames from this fire threw their light on a massive stone structure the size of a cliff. As we got closer, we saw that these were gigantic stone statues that stood side by side. The female statue had long silky black hair that reached her waistline. She was a smiling statue, with dark shiny eyes and smooth skin. Next to her stood the statue of a man. He had a kind face and seemed down-to-earth, like someone who works at the paint department of a hardware store. We were so mesmerized by this sight that we hardly noticed the many people who sat in a semicircle surrounding these titanic statues. Men and women talked among themselves, some singing, while children played games, running in and out of tents installed not in a straight line but in a semicircle, so that anyone coming out of the tent would first see the statues. The leader asked us to sit among his people.

We sat across from these statues. After a long drive of changing lanes and missing exits, it felt good just to sit on the soft cool grass, feeling the warmth of the fire. We heard some men and women making preparations for us with blankets and night lamps, chattering happily among themselves. What wonderful people were these! Sure, you get treated nicely at motels but this was more natural because they were not asking for credit-card numbers. There was no *check in* because in and out were the same for this magnificent tribe that lived in tents under the starlit sky. The heat from the fire melted the air and the statues appeared to be floating. Some children arrived with wooden bowls filled with a delicious soup of beans and meat. We ate well and then retired to the large comfortable tent they had arranged for us. On the floor were colorful quilts that invited our tired bodies to dreamland.

"Forgive me, let us decide who will sleep where…"

I couldn't have cared less. I fell on the soft colorful bed and happily sank into the world of dreams.

We must have slept well, because we woke up refreshed. The morning gave us a clear view of their way of life. I could hear music. A man sitting under a tree was playing a stringed instrument that celebrated nature. Women sat in circles, sewing pieces of cloth into large blankets. The fragrance of boiling tea leaves was in the air. A child brought us steaming towels soaked in mint water. I put my face in it and woke up my soul. We saw children with fishing rods made from sticks. They ran toward a sparkling river that flowed by their camp. Everyone who passed us did so with a smile. Was this paradise?

We had breakfast with the leader. Not the manufactured stuff, but milk, tasty goat cheese, and some bread with honey. Adnan was grateful.

"We are well rested. Our drive will be much more comfortable thanks to your hospitality."

"It is our custom to welcome a guest like family," said the leader.

"We thank you." Adnan was paying them in Thank you Dollars. Why couldn't the world work like this? The leader placed a hand on Adnan's shoulders.

"It is also our custom to take guests on our traditional hunt."

"No, thank you, we must move on," said Adnan, dipping some bread into honey.

"It is our custom," said the leader.

"We are most grateful for this generous offer, but…"

"I will make preparations," said the leader loudly, which sounded more like an order than a request.

We discussed among ourselves how to handle this situation.

"Gentlemen, I am not a hunter," said Adnan. That was not news to us. He was a man accustomed to life in the city. He had only read about hunting in books, and in movies he often fast-forwarded parts that involved the killing of living things. While he was a great admirer of biology, he liked to observe it from outside the skin.

Maaf Karna, whose ungrateful face had enjoyed the warmth of the steamy mint towel, immediately blamed Adnan. "Forgive me for saying this, but you got us into this mess."

"For one night of comfort, one night," said Hisaab Khan, holding up his forefinger like an angry principal, "you risked our lives."

"I hate to leave these generous people, but what can we do?" asked Adnan.

"Let's run away," I said.

"Forgive me," said Maaf Karna, "but that would be rude after experiencing the hospitality of these traditional people."

"Running away is not so shameless, after all," said Adnan. "It is an ancient tradition."

"Why do you say that?" asked Hisaab Khan.

"Our ancestors avoided dangerous animals by running. In war also, evasive action is accomplished by running. It is something we should not look down on when there is a higher goal in mind." Adnan quickened his pace as he spoke these words. In a few moments, we were jogging and then running wildly toward our car. We ran across the large field, made our way through the trail, but as we came near the convertible we saw members of the tribe already waiting for us.

"Ah, so eager for the hunt that you run toward the car!" said the leader. He was leaning against the bonnet with arms folded.

Adnan now used forceful words to stress that there was no way he was going on a hunt. "We are not hunters. We must decline your offer with respect."

The leader raised his right hand and his men surrounded us. Three men surrounded Maaf Karna and Hisaab Khan.

"Forgive…"

Even before he could apologize, the men grabbed Maaf Karna and Hisaab Khan by their arms and escorted them back to the camp. The leader got into the driver's seat as his men watched me and Adnan. Lowering the windows, he spoke firmly to us.

"Get in."

Hunt

"But no regret or guilt was felt by this tribe"

——————

ADNAN WAS nudged into the back seat and sandwiched by a man on each side. I tried to get out of the situation by volunteering for other duties.

"I think I will stay here and help the tribe, tidy up the logs for fire, vacuum the tents maybe, or I can help with the dishes. I'm really good with that." But the men pushed me into the passenger seat. As soon as we were all seated, the leader and his two men shouted loudly in one terrible voice.

"Let the hunt begin!"

Adnan looked pale, being one of those decent people who never kill animals but like to eat them once they are dead. As the car moved on the bumpy road, Adnan made conversation. "So, I see no weapons for hunting. How will you hunt?"

"With these," said the leader moving his fingers as if playing an imaginary piano.

Were we to hunt with our hands? How disgusting! We were not even going to hunt like civilized people who hide behind bushes and shoot bullets into unsuspecting animals. The leader took an exit toward the city.

Adnan leaned forward to talk to him, in a cheerful voice, pretending that we were all friends and going to a movie theater to watch a comedy and eat popcorn with it. "You are going towards the city. I thought we were going on a hunt?"

"We hunt in the city," said the leader with a sinister smile.

Were we going to hunt humans, because who else lives in the city? Adnan also panicked because he loves humanity and cares deeply about people, and he did not want to go to jail for the rest of his life. Gone was the friendliness and fake confidence, replaced by the sound of panic. "We request that you release us from this hunt!"

"This sucks!" I added. I think the word suck was invented for exactly this type of a situation. We were both guests and hostages to these people. We could not even abuse our tormentors because they were in complete control.

I cried.

They were amused by our panic. The leader also made things very clear.

"We are not going to release you as you have shared our tents, our food, and our trust. The rule of our hunt is that once we begin the hunt, we always end as one."

"Surely your rich traditions allow for someone to be excused from this hunt," said Adnan.

"Yes, there is one way you may be excused," said the leader.

"What is that?" I asked immediately. I was ready to do anything. Help them wash the pots and pans, remove any lint from their tents, even comb and groom the long hair on that attractive female statue.

The leader shook his head. "We were just joking! There is no way we can let you go now!"

At this sick joke the three of them laughed while Adnan and I exchanged terrified glances. We were in the city now. The leader drove into a commercial area and parked outside a Laundromat. Here, humanity had gathered to wash its clothes by using its precious quarters. The innocent fragrance of detergent and fabric softeners was in the air.

The leader got out of the car and said to his men, "Make sure our guests stay here."

The man sitting behind me placed his large rough arm around my neck as if we were best friends on a pirate ship. The leader walked into the laundromat, which had a large glass window through which we could see his evil deed. The man sitting to the left of Adnan said, "Now, watch the hunt."

Upon hearing this Adnan shouted, "Run, Minhaj, run! Get help! Go for it!"

I tried to leap out of the car but the man behind me held my neck so tightly I could do nothing. Adnan desperately tried to get out but he was elbowed back into the seat. I managed to hit the horn of the car to gain some attention. But the man behind me grabbed my hands and held them back.

"Our leader is hunting! You will scare the game!"

As we struggled against them, I saw through the large glass window what the leader was doing. At first, he walked around in the laundromat casually and then suddenly, when one of the laundry users was distracted by the mounted television, he darted toward a drying machine. He opened the dryer, and with lightning quickness he snuck his hand inside and pulled it out. This he did with several dryers while innocent humans watched television or used the vending machine to get candy with almonds with their extra quarters. He walked out of the laundromat and quickly got into the driver's seat. In silence, he drove across the street to a large parking lot outside a supermarket. Parking next to the shopping carts, he said in a voice loud and proud, "I have hunted!"

"Show us!" shouted the men from the backseat.

He produced from his pocket several socks of different colors.

"Well done, leader!" shouted his men. "First catch of the day."

"I don't understand," said Adnan. "None of these socks match. What is the point of stealing these?"

"It is not stealing," shouted the leader with anger. "We are hunters. We only hunt for one sock."

"But why?"

"It is our tradition," said the leader firmly. We did not insist on an explanation.

The rest of the day, the hunt got more daring and it is too painful to recall that we were part of something so evil. In the evening, we returned to their land. Many men were returning with bags full of socks. These they gathered in the middle of their camp grounds in front of the two smiling statues. It soon became a small colorful hill. I wondered about the many humans who had been deprived by these people. How many have done laundry only to lose a sock? Yet, they would never know where the other sock went. But no regret or guilt was felt by this tribe. In fact they celebrated their evil acts by lighting this mountain of socks on fire. As the fire burned brightly, they danced around it in a strange manner. Jumping up and down but never in coordination, they chanted:

Two minus one is one

The more you buy

The more we hunt

Two minus one is one

This chanting poetry was no doubt derived from their history as hunters of socks. Maaf Karna and Hisaab Khan joined us and informed us that they had been forced to do arts and crafts. We were once again served dinner and the people of this tribe continued to treat us like honored guests. The leader himself joined us as we slurped the tasty soup.

Adnan finally asked the leader the reason for their actions. "Why do you do this?"

The leader looked into the fire as if receiving permission from the smoldering logs. "I now reveal to you the reason for all our actions…"

Normal Sunil

"The Queen dropped a purple cloth, which was the signal"

SIX HUNDRED years ago, a normal man by the name of Sunil fell in love with a princess. So beautiful was she, it is said, that even when she stopped a yawn, her face retained beauty. Sunil wanted her hand in marriage, but there were serious cultural differences between Sunil and royalty. He worked for a living and was accountable for his actions. Despite this disadvantage, he still pursued the princess by sending her love letters and affordable jewelry.

"His most famous attempt to marry the princess came at the royal face showing. The face showing is an ancient Desi ritual. When a man reaches a marriageable age and wishes to marry a girl, he shows his face to the girl's family. If they approve of his face, then the deal is done. This, however, was a royal face showing and many wealthy bachelors (most of them with royal backgrounds) showed up at the palace. Loud royal trumpets announced the arrival of these important young men who came riding elephants and stallions with black velvet skins. Sunil arrived on foot because he could not afford a large animal upon which to sit. Only a flute that made the sound of a whistle announced his arrival.

"The face showing was held in the large royal court of the palace. On an elevated stage, sat the royal family. The king sat on his throne with his queen. They were attended by the many wise men of the court who were already whispering their opinions to one another. The princess played with her long brown hair as she reclined on a couch, her delicate frame surrounded by silk pillows. Royal guards stood in attendance with unsheathed swords, their naked arms tattooed with the royal insignia. Stringed instruments added a pleasant tune to the air. The princess lazily bathed her left hand in a bowl of rose petals. In her right hand she held a feather pen, destined to write the name of the man she would marry after the face showing.

"Each arriving bachelor was announced by a courtier. 'Here comes prince Kumar on a black stallion, lord of many lands and a thousand soldiers, a great warrior and winner of many horse riding tournaments.'

"'Here comes prince Rahul, captain of a thousand ships and master of sword fighting.'

"Sunil was also announced in the royal court. 'Sunil is here, he works for a living. At the end of the month, he pays rent.'

"The king stood up and spoke with authority. 'Let the face showing begin!'

"At this command, the musicians played their instruments. Music filled the room and the ladies of the court joined the many young bachelors on the floor. The bachelors and the royal ladies gathered in a circle to begin the dance. Sunil also found his way into the circle and stood next to a girl. The queen dropped a purple cloth, which was the signal. The musicians hit the drums and everyone in the dance circle moved to the music, skipping and moving clockwise. At first it was easy for Sunil, because circle dancing felt like teamwork. But then the queen shouted from the stage, 'Change step!' At this, the music changed. Everyone in the dance circle seemed to know what to do except for Sunil.

"Now, instead of skipping, the royal men and women were turning, bending and then jumping high into the air. This complicated dance move, which involved three steps, was accomplished easily and with pleasure by every prince and lady in the dance circle. To Sunil, it was challenging and strange. He reacted to the beat of the drum either too slowly or too quickly. He wanted to think his way through the dance and that was his tragedy. 'Okay, now I jump, now I turn' were thoughts that filled his brain. All this thinking killed his timing. Every beat of the drum was like a bird that he could never catch. He distinguished himself, but in a way that was very bad. All this while, he forced his face into a fake smile. But pain was his dance partner.

"The other men, who had done this all their lives, displayed a natural rhythm and danced gracefully, turning, twisting, and jumping. They even mocked Sunil as they did so.

"'Change step,' shouted the queen once again.

"'What? Okay!' said Sunil. But even as he expressed his surprise, the other dancers knew what to do and were already doing it. This time the dancers were required to clap in unison and then jump high into the air. Even though he very much wanted to be good at this, Sunil's body refused to accept this combination. Always, he clapped solo and then launched himself upwards a little late. When everyone was coming down he was going up. In midair he looked nervously at the other dancers, who were already on the floor and clapping. Most of them were laughing at him and not with him. Sunil realized that he was a few seconds behind. Once he was back on the floor he saw that everyone had already jumped into the air. Determined to catch up, Sunil clenched his fists and picked momentum by swinging his arms, jumping as high as he could. And as he did this, he struck the girl next to him on her chin just as she was descending. She fell to the floor and everyone was glaring at Sunil as he continued his powerful journey upwards. The music stopped.

"At this moment, Sunil did not want to come down. But gravity made sure he did. He landed back on the floor with a thump and clapped twice loudly, with the hope that this innovation would be received with some appreciation.

"'What have you done?' said the queen from the stage. 'You are spoiling it for everyone. You hurt that girl so badly. Accept your defeat and go home, for this is not your place and you are most unwanted.'

"Just then the princess got up, walked over to the king and handed him a piece of paper. The king turned the paper and on it was written 'Sunil.'

"'Sunil?' gasped the king. 'Have you lost your royal mind?' The whole court was in shock and some screamed in horror.

"But the princess had chosen. She spoke with great wisdom. 'Anyone who dances that badly and still refuses to leave the dance floor is the bravest man of all. I shall belong to him. Brave Sunil, you may kiss my hand and win me as your bride.'

"The royal court panicked. They had devised the royal face showing to keep out normal people like Sunil. Now, it had backfired. As Sunil walked towards the princess climbing up the stage his pants shifted upwards revealing his socks.

"'Wait!' said the queen. 'Your socks! They do not match!'

"Sunil looked down and realized that he had not matched his socks. Wanting to make an excellent impression, he had focused too much on his upper body, oiling his hair, shaving his jaw, making his ears squeaky clean. But in his excitement, he had worn a maroon sock on his one foot and a yellow sock on the other.

"'It's not a big deal,' said Sunil in his most confident voice. 'It happens all the time.'

"'We reject you,' said the queen. 'You have no sense of symmetry.'

"'You have broken the laws of the land, and therefore we disqualify you from the face showing,' said the king.

"'Is there a law that forbids a man from wearing two different socks?' asked Sunil.

"'There is now,' said the king, using his authority in the most unjust manner. 'Guards, throw this man out!'

"Sunil went home confused, but also angry that such a small thing would separate him from the love of his life. Some palace slaves and bad dancers supported Sunil and felt he had been wronged. They helped Sunil sneak into the palace to meet the princess.

"'I was too excited, and did not bother to match my socks,' he explained to the princess.

"She believed him, and that very night they ran away together into the wild.

"Their first few months away from civilization were happy. They honeymooned at a nearby cliff, eating bread and counting stars in the night sky in made up languages to amplify feelings of romance. They played simple games like *guess in which hand I have a stone?* But it got old because there were only two possibilities. The princess missed her people and the liveliness of palace life. But they could not go back because the court had banished them. Feeling the pain of this treatment, the loving couple vowed that they would make the world understand. They told their story to anyone who would listen.

"They placed a sign in front of their tent:

"*Your socks need not match. Even if you have no rhythm, you are welcome, because you exist.*'

"Some visitors felt so welcome that they never left. The tents grew in number, and they became known as the tribe of Missisoka. We are their descendants."

The leader pointed to the two statues, which smiled upon us with a new familiarity. I noticed that the male statue wore different colored socks on each foot. It was normal Sunil. He was the honored one.

"They are our ancestors," said the leader with reverence. "We honor their memory by dancing badly around the fire.

We go on hunts. By taking away one sock from the people, we force them to wear socks that do not match. Only then will they know what our great ancestor, normal Sunil, experienced. We change the world, one sock at a time."

We sat staring at the fire for a few minutes. The leader left us and mingled with his people. We were free to go. As we left their grounds, Maaf Karna and Hisaab Khan complained about the whole experience. Adnan, who usually loved to analyze other cultures and their complexities, remained silent. There was a reason for this. That day, along with the leader and other men, we too had joined them. Adnan had snuck into another laundromat and grabbed a blue-and-yellow striped sock and I, a polka-dotted beauty. We had hunted, and that thrill was impossible to explain.

"*What have you done!*"

⎯⎯⎯◆⎯⎯⎯

I N THE mountainous state of Tennessee we stopped for fuel. The lady at the cash register was in a cheerful mood, offering us free coffee. A group of woman joggers ran past the gas station at an impressive pace. At an intersection a policewoman guided traffic, smiling at us. We drove past a showroom filled with shiny sports cars. Through the glass walls we could see the saleswomen talking enthusiastically to their female customers.

"Women have made great strides and have joined the work force," said Adnan.

"Forgive me, but where are the men?" asked Maaf Karna.

"We have not seen one man since we got into this town," said Hisaab Khan. "The cashier at the gas station was a woman, we saw women jogging, the traffic police was a woman, and all the drivers I see on the road are women. All this goes against the laws of probability."

"I'm sure that is just a coincidence," said Adnan. He pointed to a mechanic's garage that was coming up. "We are probably going to see men in that mechanic shop."

Maaf Karna slowed the car as we passed the garage. We looked in, and a long-haired woman in blue overalls, holding a wrench, stared back at us.

"See that!" said Hisaab Khan. "There are no men in this town!"

"Just a coincidence," maintained Adnan, but I could tell that he was not completely convinced. We stopped at a red light. Hisaab Khan was explaining to us how probability works when we saw a young man crossing the street.

"There goes a man!" said Adnan. "This town is not so strange after all. We should never jump to..." But even before he could finish, the young man crossing the street fell to the ground. We got out of the car and ran toward this fallen man. He was a young man, in his early twenties; he lay on the street with his eyes closed. We threw water on his face, which brought him back to consciousness.

"Where am I?" he said in a weak voice.

Adnan made a V sign with his two fingers. "Tell me, how many fingers do you see?"

"Seven," said the young man, his lips barely moving.

"You are not well," concluded Adnan. Hisaab Khan held the young man's head and fed him more water which he drank with his quivering lips. He gained strength and spoke with more clarity.

"My name is Faizan. My home is nearby. Please take me home."

We picked him up and carried him to the car. He was surprisingly light for a young man, like an empty box of pizza. In his shaky, soft voice, he guided us to his home. I rang the bell, and a man with graying hair opened the front door.

"Father," said Faizan, "these people found me at the walk signal."

"Oh, is that where you fainted?" asked his father.

"Has this happened before?" asked Adnan.

"Of course," said the father with a very normal smile, as if fainting was something people did all the time.

We found this strange but helped Faizan make his way into the house. It was a beautiful home, almost like a museum, with many paintings on the walls and a large bookshelf filled with romance novels. A glass window on the roof allowed plenty of sunlight to fall on the white marble floor. Faizan's mother, a round and healthy-looking woman, joined us.

"What happened?"

"Your son collapsed while crossing the road," said Adnan. "I think you should call a doctor."

"Forget it," she said showing no signs of worry. "He will be fine." She looked at Faizan and said, "There is some soup in the kitchen. Go drink that."

Faizan, looking dizzy, wobbled his way to the kitchen.

Adnan introduced himself to the parents in an official manner. "I am Adnan Raheem Khan, president of the Desi League. These gentlemen are in the governing council. We are on our way to Washington, DC."

"Yes, I saw your letter in *Hi There News*. You are doing a good thing for the Desis."

This delighted Adnan because it was the first time he was recognized for his writing. "Thank you! It's good to know that the people are behind us."

"We support you. The Desis need a voice," said Faizan's father. "We are about to attend a wedding. Would you like to join us? You could meet more Desis over there and explain your political views."

"Forgive us, but we really must be on our way," said Maaf Karna looking at Adnan for support.

"We would love to join you for lunch at the wedding," said Adnan.

We used their home to shower and put on fresh clothes for the wedding. Soon we were on our way, following their station wagon to the wedding venue.

In the privacy of our car, Maaf Karna expressed what was on all our minds. "Forgive me for saying this, but the boy faints, and they don't care!"

"Yes," said Hisaab Khan, "Faizan thinks two is seven, he needs help."

"Yes," said Adnan. "I am going to have a talk with his father."

"There are four of us showing up at a wedding, and we are not even taking a gift for them," said Hisaab Khan.

"We are rewarding them with the gift of our company, gentlemen. That should be enough. But before we go in, we should know the names of the bride and groom so that we don't appear rude."

"Will there be cake?" I asked.

No one answered my question, but from their faces I could see they wished for it. I was not curious about who was getting married. I was just glad that they were, because wedding meals are tasty.

We arrived at the wedding, where two large tents had been erected, one for the men and one for the women. Faizan's mother went to the women's tent and the rest of us were greeted by the father of the groom, who stood at the entrance of the men's tent. Entering this magnificent white tent was a nice feeling. The ground was carpeted with thick maroon carpets. Large chandeliers hung from the roof, round tables were covered with crisp white cloth, and in the center of each table stood a bouquet of fresh roses. Cheerful music was playing, and we happily took our seats at one of the round tables.

Sitting on a stage facing all the tables was the groom dressed in a white suit. The backdrop of the stage was a wall of raw-silk cloth covered with colorful flowers. At our table, Adnan used this opportunity to lecture everyone on the benefits of education and the spreading of knowledge. Faizan was nodding politely but also yawning. Adnan would have been more effective if he did not begin all his lectures, "From the dawn of time." Finally, I saw the catering staff moving around, putting the plates on the serving tables. The clatter of plates and the soft thud of glasses being placed on cloth-covered tables further tantalized our senses. Adnan was still lecturing us, and had reached the Stone Age in his chronological seminar. Finally the groom's father came to us.

"Dinner is served. Please begin," he said with polite hospitality. I really love these moments when an extremely boring time is shaken up by the announcement of food. However, in Desi culture, it is always decent at weddings to show some reluctance when invited to eat. We are supposed to pretend that we did not hear the invitation by continuing to talk to each other even though our stomachs are screaming for food. This is to be followed by an expression of surprise, such as "oh, there is food here?"

I rushed toward the serving table and grabbed a plate. What I saw on the serving table shocked my hungry body. In one dish were carrots, and in the other dish were cabbage leaves. Coffee was also being served. I thought that perhaps this was the salad area and the real food would arrive soon. I asked one of the caterers when the real meal was arriving.

"This is the main course," he said. "Please enjoy."

Enjoy? Was he crazy? Carrots and cabbage leaves with coffee! I could not believe this! After enduring a day with this strange family and their fainting boy, we were being treated like rabbits. I saw Adnan, placing carrots on his plate while he continued his lecture, which had now reached the agricultural revolution. I walked out of the tent to get some fresh air. On my way out, I caught a glimpse of the women's tent. Dinner had been served to them as well. But how different was their destiny!

In large bronze pans heated by fire were roasted chicken, mashed potatoes, and gravy. Also being served to them were fresh, piping-hot breads of all kinds. Though it would be considered rude to go into their tent, I could not resist. I wanted this real food. I entered the women's tent. On the stage facing the round tables sat the bride. But unlike the groom, she was laughing loudly. There was in her not a hint of anxiety.

Eastern brides often display emotion, even sadness, at leaving their old life behind. But this bride was happily biting into a leg of chicken. In front of the stage some other girls danced aggressively, cell phones in hand, drinking soda straight from the glass bottles without the use of straws. Other women were whistling and being rowdy.

I was enraged that these women were enjoying a menu from the heavens. And what did we get? Leaves and carrots. I get daring when I am hungry. When no one was looking, I ran toward their food table, grabbed a plate, and put several pieces of chicken on it. I also went for all the bread I could fit on my plate, and then quickly I ran out without anyone noticing. I returned to the men's tent feeling victorious, holding this treasure of food on my plate. At least I was going to have a decent meal. I was about to sit down when I saw that all the men were staring at me as I stood there with the plate full of chicken and tasty dinner rolls.

"They have better food in the other tent," I said, attempting to kill the awkwardness of the moment.

The groom's father seemed the most disturbed. He slapped his forehead with both hands. "What have you done?"

I felt he was overreacting. Sure, I had gone into the women's tent, but it wasn't as if I had done anything too wrong, and the women were not at all shy. So I did not understand what the big deal was.

Then, it happened.

A young man standing near me fell to the ground. And then another young man fell. One by one, they were all collapsing! Even the groom, who was on the stage, fainted and fell from his sofa.

Guilt

"Everyone was staring at me using their eyes to throw lasers of guilt"

THE OLDER men were screaming. "Call the women, call the women. We need help!"

Two women rushed into our tent and ran toward me like I was a rugby ball. The one who reached me first snatched the plate from my hands and gave it to the other woman, who ran out of the tent with it. More women had rushed into our tent. They quickly took charge as the men watched helplessly, huddled together in a corner. The women picked up the young men, slung them over their shoulders, and carried them out of the tent.

"We are going to drive these men to the hospital," said one of the women.

The groom's father glared at me. "You have ruined the best day of my son's life." He helped a woman place his son in the back seat of a sports car. Faizan's father came to me and said, "You have embarrassed us deeply. I am going to the hospital to apologize for your behavior. The least you can do is come to the hospital."

We were soon in our car and following them to the hospital.

"This is all so strange," said Adnan. Maaf Karna and Hisaab Khan were, as usual, blaming me. Guilt combined with hunger inside my body to create a new kind of sadness. At the emergency ward, we watched as the young men were placed on stretchers. We saw Faizan being taken away, an oxygen mask on his face. We sat with the elders in the waiting area. Everyone was staring at me, their eyes throwing lasers of guilt. It was a difficult time. I mostly looked at the ceiling, which I felt was also judging me with spotlights.

After a long wait, a doctor arrived to give us the news. "They are going to be fine."

Everyone was relieved. They shook hands among themselves, thanking merciful God but not forgiving me. The groom's father was too angry to see me. But Adnan, on my behalf, apologized for my behavior. He approached the attending physician, a dark-haired woman in a white lab coat.

"Doctor why did this happen? Why did the men faint?"

"You are not from around here I see," she said. "Come with me."

We followed her to the cafeteria and she told us the story over a cup of hot chocolate and German chocolate cake.

"We trace the fall of man back to a beauty contest," she said, stirring the melting whipped cream as it sank into the hot chocolate. "For many years, women competed with each other over who could be the prettiest. The girl who won this competition would win a special place in our city parade. One year, it was decided that men would also compete in the beauty contest."

"It's only natural to want to compete," said Adnan.

"Nature is a tricky thing," said the doctor. "The beauty contest became very important and men, who are by nature highly competitive, began to look at all the remedies that women had traditionally applied to win. They hired life coaches, placed sliced cucumbers on their eyes, moisturized their skins with exotic muds from all over the world."

"Forgive me, but all this sounds harmless," said Maaf Karna.

"In those days being slim was a large part of being beautiful, so the men competed to lose as much weight as possible. At first, they did so with exercise."

"Sounds healthy," said Adnan.

"Healthy," said the doctor with a mocking smile. "It was healthy until they got this crazy idea that bread would make them fat. And here was this conflict in their nature."

"Forgive me, but what conflict?" asked Maaf Karna, getting curious.

"This desire to win at all costs. But in order to win they had to give up bread. The winner of the first men's beauty contest said in his acceptance speech that avoiding bread was his secret to victory."

"What a freak!" I said.

"Let's not judge," said Adnan. "This kind of thing still happens."

The doctor broke a piece of chocolate cake as she continued. "It soon became fashionable for men to be very slim, and in their attempts to achieve the ideal weight they gave up eating bread."

"Forgive me, but that is insanity," said Maaf Karna, who loved bread.

"Yes, it was," said the doctor with a dry laugh. "Avoiding bread led to mental problems, and men lost their ability to make decisions. They became weak. At times they were unable to pick up things, including themselves. The women, on the other hand, had been drinking smoothies, and this had vitalized their strength, because strawberries and bananas contain iron and calcium. Soon it came to be that if a man fainted on the street due to a lack of carbs, a woman would pick him up and carry him to a hospital. Things reached a stage where male helplessness was romanticized as something attractive. Animated films such as *The Fainting Beauty* were released in 3D. A famous song that stayed number one on the radio charts was called *"Faint on Me."* Fashion designers created clothes for men with handles, so that when they fainted, women could pick them up with ease. Being incompetent, not being able to do things, asking for help came to define men."

"So this is why we saw only women when we drove into town?" asked Adnan.

"With the fall of men, a power vacuum was created," said the doctor, enjoying her chocolate cake, "especially for those jobs that require the use of memory and movement. Women became the breadwinners, eating the bread, while the men, avoiding the eating of it, became weaker and financially dependent on them."

"So that's why we saw so many board games and romance novels at Faizan's house. He hardly ever leaves the house!" said Adnan.

"Yes," said the doctor and sipped her hot chocolate. "Due to the possibility of fainting, men stay mostly at home watching films that are terribly sad but oddly satisfying to them. The women meanwhile, who had made great mental and physical progress, went to the gym and held meetings in tall buildings, smoking cigars, and discussing the stock market. For lunch, the women ate healthy sandwiches because time was less and sandwich was convenient."

"Fascinating!" said Adnan. "But let me ask you doctor, why don't the men eat bread now?"

"Their system rejects it," said the doctor. "Psychologically they are convinced that they will cease to be men if they eat bread. Which is why when your friend here," she looked at me, "showed up with loaves of bread on his plate, the young men could not handle it. It was too much for them. Like whiskey to a baby who only knows milk."

We were too stunned to speak. We left the hospital and got out of that town as soon as we could.

On the highway, I finally broke the silence. "Is anyone hungry?"

"How about a nothing sandwich?" said Hisaab Khan, keeping his eyes on the road but his anger toward me.

"Forgive me, but that is exactly what he deserves," said Maaf Karna, as if our car was a courtroom and he was the appointed judge.

But there was no denying that this incident had shaken us. We stopped at a magnificent grocery store with a large clock tower. Adnan bought more bread than we could fit in the car. And as we rode toward Virginia, we ate all kinds: seven grain, Italian, sourdough, whole wheat, rye, that long French one... We were grateful for every bite.

"Do you know why I am good?"

———————◆———————

WE WERE in Virginia, cruising on Route 66, a historic American highway built through lands that had seen war, love, and daily traffic jams. The traffic slowed down and finally came to a halt because of some fire engines that were blocking the highway. Smoke was rising from an area outside a commercial building.

The office workers had exited the building. There was a ring of fire around the building as if an arsonist had set it by design. Maaf Karna turned off the engine and we got out of the car to stretch our legs. We saw a man in gray trousers and a white shirt walking away from the building. Adnan struck up a conversation.

"What happened here?" asked Adnan.

The man seemed eager to talk and introduced himself. "My name is Literal Desi. My friends call me LD."

"Nice to meet you, LD. My name is Adnan, and we are on our way to Washington, DC, to represent the Desis."

He was delighted to hear these words. "I love Washington, DC. Everything is exactly what it is named. The White House is white, the Pentagon has five sides. I know they have a Chinatown, where they serve egg drop soup. It is made exactly as they say—by dropping an egg into the soup."

"You are a straightforward man," observed Adnan.

"I am sir. Washington, DC, is only twenty miles from here. Can you take me there? I would like to visit the National Museum of Natural History. I love looking at the dinosaur bones."

"It will be my pleasure," said Adnan. He always loved it when anyone displayed any sort of curiosity for things of the past. "You may come with us."

"Forgive me, but we hardly know this man," said Maaf Karna.

But Adnan would hear nothing of it. "Don't be silly Maaf, he is a good boy."

The traffic cleared, and soon we were on our way with Literal Desi sitting between me and Hisaab Khan in the back.

"When you said that I am a good boy, you were absolutely right." said LD.

"I am sure you are," said Adnan. "It's difficult to find young people these days filled with a wonder for the past." LD leaned forward to ask Adnan a strange question.

"Do you know why I am good?"

"Why?"

"Because I always do what I am told. Like today at work. At a meeting we were told to create a firewall for our company so that no one from outside could access our files. The other lazy, corrupt workers were not following orders. So I did it. You saw my work."

"What do you mean?" asked Adnan.

"The fire that you saw. I did that."

"But a firewall is computer software that protects files from unauthorized access!"

"No, sir. It is a wall of fire."

And then it struck us. Literal Desi took everything literally.

"By fire wall they meant a software program!" Adnan was shouting. "I have never been good at computers but even I know that!"

Literal Desi had lost his approval rating among us. Adnan was highly agitated because he realized that in our car was an arsonist who had joined us by his own request.

But Literal Desi was even angrier at the suggestion that fire wall meant software. "You are a liar," he shouted back.

"It's called language!" said Adnan. "It's full of words that have double meanings and phrases. When people want to wish actors good luck, they say, 'Break a leg.' This is not a request for fracture."

But Literal Desi refused to understand.

"It is people like you with their fancy words and confusing ideas that have destroyed this world. This is why I like dinosaurs. They were pure. They had big jaws and they ate other animals. No hypocrisy."

"Forgive me, but I think you are romanticizing," said Maaf Karna, jumping in.

"No, I am not. They chased and ate animals. They were frank and decent creatures. Not like this Mr. Adnan who says one thing and means another."

"But do animals not use deception and cunning when they hunt?" asked Adnan. "Like the lion that hides behind tall grass as we have observed in nature documentaries?"

"Silence your mouths, you hypocrites," said Literal Desi. He then punched the roof. "I once waited four hours at a zebra crossing but the exotic animals never showed up. I can't stand you liars. Stop the car right now at the next metro station. I want nothing to do with you."

Feelings were most definitely mutual.

Maaf quickly took the exit for the metro station. There was a lot of tension in the car. Literal Desi was different, and yet there was something frank and honest about him.

Adnan continued with his lecture. "Fact is, LD, that one thing can have many meanings. We must accept this to survive in this world."

"Stop the car right here," said Literal Desi. We were outside the metro station and Maaf Karna stopped the car. Literal Desi got out and ran into the station. We were barely recovering from this argument when we heard a man scream.

"How dare you!"

The sign outside the Vienna metro station had the words "*Kiss & Ride*".

"From the caveman to the space age, the accomplishments of humanity invite our attention"

HIGHWAY 66 curved, leaving behind the practical world of apartments and gas stations; then straightening again, it brought us face-to-face with the imperial city. The highway was now a bridge crossing over a magnificent river that flowed beneath us. Cruising on this bridge high above the river we felt like we were flying into the city. Something beautiful was visible beyond the river. Limestone pillars arranged in a circle supported a cream-colored dome that drank sunlight and glowed like a pearl against the blue sky. It was a place where Hercules might do his morning workouts. Directly in front of us rose a cluster of ancient white stone buildings, and from among these emerged a gigantic tower pointing to the sky.

We entered Constitution Avenue, a wide road bordered by tall and friendly trees and dignified buildings that lifted our spirits with their Greek pillars and maroon tiles adorning their sloping roofs. Faces of gods greeted us with their marble eyes. Statues of wise men and powerful women in flowing robes graced the rooftops, calling our attentions to higher things like justice, courage, and not being lazy. We parked and walked past the Washington Monument, which stands like a massive stone needle pointing to the sky.

"This monument is five hundred fifty-five feet, five and one-eighth inches high," said Hisaab Khan. We stood in the rectangular garden that has the Washington Monument at one end and on the other end, the pastry-colored Capitol building.

The many museums and galleries got Adnan very excited. "These buildings hold cultural treasures, gentlemen. From the caveman to the space age, the accomplishments of humanity invite our attention."

He walked toward an elegant stone building not very high but in harmony with its surroundings. It had the words *"Freer Gallery of Art"* engraved at the entrance. We pushed the heavy glass door open and entered. Ancient statues of fierce warriors, carved doors that had once guarded secrets in palaces, azure-colored tea vessels used on a lively night a thousand years ago—such things surrounded us. In one section, inside a glass box, lay a large gleaming dagger. Intricate carvings like tiny rivers of gold covered both the handle and the blade. The caption beneath it: *"At dawn a tremendous noise arose in the east. It was so terrifying that it nearly frightened the inhabitants out of their skins. Then, in the midst of tumultuous noise, something bright fell to the earth from above…"*

These were the words of an Indian king who was describing a glittering meteorite that had fallen into his kingdom. The king had extracted metal from it to create the dagger we now saw before us.

Adnan stood in front of the dagger reading these words slowly. Then he remarked almost to himself, "We all have our weapons, don't we?"

"Forgive me, but what do you mean?"

But Adnan seemed to be in a hurry and ignored Maaf Karna's question.

"I must go. Let's meet in front of the Capitol in one hour." He walked away quickly and left us standing among these ancient things. We all wondered the same thing. The pressure of facing Senator Neverist was getting to him.

Senator

"Television, radio and the newspapers had given him that same larger-than-life quality we attribute to movie stars"

IN THE art gallery, standing among strange and wonderful things, we forgot time. When we did remember, we were already late. We rushed out of the gallery and walked quickly on the long rectangular garden toward Capitol Hill. The Capitol building is much farther than it appears. Perhaps that's the beauty of it. To a pedestrian it looks intimate and friendly and makes you forget the distance you must travel to reach it. At the end of the rectangular garden is a street, which we crossed and reached a large round lake. Beyond this lake stands a statue of General Grant on a horse as if he is guarding Capitol Hill. It was beneath that statue that a small crowd was gathered and among them was our leader, Adnan Raheem Khan. In his hands he held a black briefcase.

"Gentlemen, look at these statues," he said pointing to the statues of four lions that surrounded General Grant. Four lions! I ask you—how many are we?"

"We are four," I said getting excited.

"A sign!" said Adnan.

But Maaf Karna was not impressed. "Forgive me, but what are you going to say to the senator? And why do you have that briefcase?"

Our conversation was disturbed by the sound of clapping. Senator Neverist had arrived. Photographers ran to take up their positions. Television, radio, and the newspapers had given him that larger-than-life quality we attribute to movie stars. Standing in front of the beautiful Capitol building, which appealed to man's higher senses, was this man and his petty agenda. He spoke in his husky voice into a microphone.

"I am here to start a nationwide campaign against the extra privileges enjoyed by the Desis."

Adnan moved forward toward the senator.

"Senator," he shouted. "I want to speak with you."

A man belonging to the senator's staff came and stood in front of Adnan.

"Sorry," he said with no hint of apology. "The senator is addressing the country right now. He is not available to you."

"But I live in the country!"

"Yes, don't we all? Why don't you write him an e-mail? Then our webmaster can put it in the trash folder and then empty the recycle bin, so we never have to deal with your thoughts again."

The senator was now addressing his audience of loyal supporters and members of the press.

"I would like to reaffirm my commitment to the values that we hold dear in America. Today I will launch a countrywide movement against the Desi marriage laws. I will be traveling in a private jet with a personal chef and a masseuse all over the country so I can spend time with decent, hardworking Americans. I will be talking about these terrible laws that are making life unbearable for us."

Adnan shouted again, "Senator!"

The political aide to the senator glared at Adnan. "This is a press statement. You are disturbing the peace!"

"Then you leave me no choice," said Adnan. He put the black briefcase in front of him on the floor and sat down to open it. Near the handle of the suitcase was a digital panel displaying numbers in red.

Adnan flipped opened the briefcase. Intense heat and smoke came out of it. The numbers on the display panel were now counting backward, *99, 98, 97.* I felt a whiff of heat and saw Adnan's smiling face surrounded by steamy smoke.

A security guard shouted, "He has a device! Everyone get away!"

Heat

"In the middle of the smoke stood Adnan"

⁓

THE GOD-FEARING senator was the first to run, and the press conference became a commotion with security guards bumping into cameramen who were also trying to get as far away from Adnan as possible. In the middle of the smoke stood Adnan holding a gleaming silver disc over his head as if offering it to the sky. I realized that these were naans (hot Desi bread) wrapped in aluminum foil.

"Come, let us eat," said Adnan. He looked at us as if everything was normal. It was a dramatic way to announce lunch, but it did get everyone's attention.

"Forgive me, but that is the most sinister looking picnic basket the world has ever seen," said Maaf Karna.

"I like that it counts," said Hisaab Khan. "The display panel shows the temperature of this box that keeps the food hot."

Naans are round, hot, paper-thin breads, crispy on the outside and chewy on the inside. They can be eaten with anything. As the fragrance of these hot naans filled the air we were surrounded by birds. A spiritual scene occurred when a bird came and sat on the shoulder of our great leader, Adnan Raheem Khan, as he took the chaplee kebabs from the hot box. Chaplee kebabs are spicy disks of fried meat upon which slices of tomato and green chili melt into a happy union. The smoke particles from these kebabs danced with the air molecules of Washington, DC. Senator Neverist turned around and said, "What is this fragrance that tickles our nostrils and seduces our senses?"

We, the Desi League, sat down in front of the lion statues. I then took out the karahee chicken from a box. Karahee chicken is a mixture of onions, garlic, Desi spices, tomatoes and hot oil. As the chicken floats in a mixture of spicy oil, it sends a message that few can resist. We were about to break bread and I was shocked to see the many people who stood around us. Tourists who had come to see the city, politicians whom I had only seen on TV, and yes, the very senator who had so vehemently opposed our laws. With him were birds, and wild animals. Adnan continued to eat as if he were at home eating on his couch. Sometimes he would pause and say something like, "Can you please pass me the hot naan, which is slightly crisp on the outside but soft on the inside?"

His every request described the food in great detail and made me extremely hungry.

"Can you please pass me the crisp onions that I will add to the chicken gravy to add zest to this scrumptious meal?"

I joined him in his descriptions. "Here you go, great leader. May I also give you some sizzling chicken karahee so that you can combine it with the naan?"

Maaf Karna joined in. "Forgive me for saying this, but this food is the best I have ever eaten. The kebab is melting in my mouth."

"On a scale of one to ten," said Hisaab Khan, "I give it a ten."

Finally the senator could not take it anymore. "Oh, if I could only eat these tasty things with you!"

"Please join us, senator," said Adnan, which invited shouts of excitement from the press. Adnan had invited to our picnic the very man who was working day and night to make life difficult for the Desis. Senator Neverist sat down next to Adnan, keeping his eyes on the hot box.

Adnan spoke from a position of authority. "The food you are about to experience is spicy. I demand that you send one of your political aides to get us cans of ice-cold soda."

The senator immediately turned around to the man who had stopped Adnan at the press conference. "You heard him. Do it!"

At his order, the political aide ran toward a street vendor.

I handed Senator Neverist a paper plate which he received gratefully with both hands. The press photographers took a picture of this very moment, the senator holding the paper plate. One of the reporters spoke into a camera.

Senator Neverist was expected to announce a nationwide tour to promote opposition to the Desi marriage laws. Instead we are now seeing the senator sharing a picnic with a man who claims to be the president of the Desi League. The senator has also sent one of his political aides to get cold cans of soda.

Adnan placed a chaplee kebab on the senator's plate.

"May I have some naan as well?" asked the Senator. "It is not complete without the naan."

For someone who had opposed the Desis with so much vigor, the senator seemed to know a lot about Desi food. I pulled a naan out of the aluminum foil and the Senator grabbed it. He broke the naan with one hand using his thumb and forefinger like an expert. He did not need the fork, using the piece of naan to scoop a bite of chaplee kebab into his mouth. As these tasty things entered his mouth, his face glowed with a spontaneous delight seldom seen on the face of a politician.

"Oh, this is so good!"

"Yes it is, Senator," said Adnan. "Eat." And then sensing his moment, Adnan asked him the most direct question.

"Senator, why do you speak out against the Desis when your love for our food is evident in your actions?"

"It was Ahmed," cried the Senator as he gulped down the whole chaplee kebab. "We went to high school together. Everyday after school I would go to his house after our chess club meetings. His mother cooked. We used to watch science fiction movies on the VCR. But after high school Ahmed went to a different college."

"Did you stay in touch with Ahmed?" asked Adnan as the press, the politicians, birds, and animals watched this amazing interview.

"Sometimes I got a postcard from him."

"So your best friend was a Desi?"

"Yes."

The press went wild, shouting questions and snapping pictures. But Adnan kept his focus on the senator who continued with his astounding story.

"But when he got married he didn't invite me to his wedding. Oh, how they must have eaten at his wedding! I was so angry. I decided to stay away from all Desis. I even gave up on Desi restaurants."

"Oh what a terrible thing," said Adnan.

"Yes," said the senator. "But as you know, once you have tasted Desi food the craving never leaves you. It grew inside of me. I became a madman. I jogged, I swam, I even joined a fitness gym. I did Latin cardio, salsa, but nothing could make me forget! I ate chicken salad sandwiches and casseroles, you know, the western stuff...but my tongue had tasted chaplee kebab. Western food made no sense."

"What did you do then?" asked Adnan.

"My hunger I turned into anger. I hated what I had once loved. I declared war on Desi culture, which had both seduced and rejected me. I felt if I could somehow remove every sight and every smell of your food, I would be free from it."

Now Adnan unleashed his greatest weapon. "Minhaj, open that box," he ordered like a commanding general who is also a statesman and an excellent picnic partner. He was pointing to the only unopened tray of food. It was covered with aluminum foil. Just as I pulled back the aluminum foil, Senator Neverist shouted like a child meeting Santa not in some artificial mall setting but on the North Pole.

"Oh my God, is that really what I think it is?"

"Yes," said Adnan. "It is nihari."

Nihari, tender pieces of meat submerged in a meat stew of oil and hot spices, all made tastier by the addition of lemon.

I saw tears in the eyes of Senator Neverist. Tears of joy. Adnan used a large spoon and poured the nihari into a bowl. He further squeezed some lemon on it and sprinkled chopped pieces of ginger. The cold cans of soda had arrived and Maaf Karna was opening the cans and handing them out. The *tish tish* of the cans opening, the combined fragrance of nihari, kebabs, lemon, and naans, the gentle breeze, the brilliant blue sky above us, and joyful beating of all our hearts compelled the senator to love life and his fellow man. He redeemed himself in one moment of sincerity.

"I denounce my ways and shall be your loyal ally. Can you please pass me the nihari?"

The reporters expressed shock by shouting questions at the senator. One of the reporters got so excited he climbed a nearby tree and reported from there because he got a better view. They were snapping pictures of the senator as he broke a piece of naan and dipped into the steaming-hot nihari. The naan absorbed the nihari and glistened like gold holding in it all the flavors discovered by human civilization.

As he placed this nihari-soaked naan into his mouth the senator's face displayed an Olympian calm, something we might see on the faces of ancient Greek gods. Truly he was on Olympus.

"I am so high right now," he said.

He furiously continued to eat the nihari and then simply lay down on the grass. Staring at the clouds above, he loosened his belt and closed his eyes.

The reporters rushed toward the senator. His security personnel were most concerned.

"What has happened to him? Should we call an ambulance?"

"No," said Adnan. "I have sent him to heaven."

At this there was great shouting and a policeman wanted to arrest Adnan. Then one of the political aides demanded clarification.

"Heaven? What do you mean? Is he dead? Have you killed him?"

"No, unlike people of other nations, Desis don't have to die to go to heaven."

"That is impossible! How can you avoid the procedure? Step one die, step two heaven! That's how it works!"

"We bypass that."

"How?"

"Because we have oil," said Adnan. "The food we eat is so loaded with it, the spices so powerful, that it takes us to the highest level. After eating, we experience a spiritual drowsiness in which things from this world become blurry, and chubby angels lift us to heaven."

"Is the senator going to be okay?"

"Yes, he will wake up in two hours, but don't expect him to do any work. For the rest of the day he will roll around from here to there with a lazy smile on his face."

"It seems you have used some kind of diabolical scheme to turn the senator into your slave."

"We are all slaves to nihari," said Adnan. He pointed to the senator, who slept peacefully with a smile of an innocent child.

Adnan then raised his voice so that all the reporters could hear him. "This senator who lies napping before you led a movement against the Desi laws. He even said Desi weddings must stop. But we cannot do that. Desis are a marriage-based culture. Without these functions we cannot function. It is our basic right. By asking us to stop our marriage traditions, you are asking the pharaoh to break the pyramid."

Adnan Raheem Khan, our great leader, had achieved complete victory. It was our finest moment. Yet.

"*Here is your victory*"

ALL THE way back to Dallas, our excitement level remained high.

I had the highest expectations. "Do you think the Desis will arrange a dance of joy for us? Will they form two lines, one of men and one of women? Shall we walk in between them showered by rose petals? Will I be stopped by beautiful girls at happy intervals so they can tell me how grateful they are to me?"

"Forgive me for saying this, but you are being a little too optimistic," said Maaf Karna but even he couldn't bring us down.

"Yes, Minhaj. Don't expect too much," said Adnan, but even he had expectations. "I am sure they will just throw a dinner in our honor and I will be interviewed by some local journalists. Perhaps some will want my autograph...but that is not why we serve."

As we entered the city of Dallas, we felt like Roman emperors returning from a successful campaign. We were almost out of gas so we stopped at the same store from which Adnan purchased extra-large sodas.

The cashier refused to recognize Adnan and even said, "Your card has been declined." Hisaab Khan had some cash on him and made the payment. Our mood was not dampened by this because we were returning home victorious.

As we pulled into the driveway of Adnan's house, we were greeted by silence. There was no welcome committee, no photographers. No beautiful, grateful girls greeted us. There was only one person. Adnan's wife, Naureen. She was standing at the front door with her arms folded, and her face displayed negative excitement.

"I thought you were going to DC for work. But I saw you on TV eating kebabs on Capitol Hill."

Adnan was too elated by his great victory. "So you witnessed the success of our mission!"

"Here is your victory," said Naureen, handing Adnan a newspaper.

Desi Man Claims to be Pharaoh: Asks America to Worship Him—A Special Report

Yesterday the Capitol Hill press conference was disturbed by a rowdy gang of protesters who belong to a group who call themselves the Desi League. Their leader, Mr. Adnan Raheem Khan, who has been arrested before for reckless driving and for being drunk on joy, was seen carrying a suspicious looking briefcase near Capitol Hill. From this briefcase he produced food that our investigators now believe was too powerful for the human body to sustain a state of wakefulness. After eating this food, Senator Neverist fell into a deep sleep and did not wake up till the next morning. Ignoring the reporters, the senator went straight to a local kebab house and told the reporters that he now "lives to eat" and has "lost all interest in politics." Mr. Adnan Raheem Khan is unemployed and suffers from megalomania. He also lied to his wife about his trip to Washington, DC.

"Great men serve humanity at the cost of domestic bliss"

———————

THE NEXT morning Adnan called a meeting in his office. We sat facing him as he read aloud the news report describing our actions in Washington, DC. "For a paper called *Hi There News* they really are negative."

If this report was bad, the mood in the house was even worse. Adnan's wife interrupted our meeting by walking into the study and throwing a stack of papers on the table.

"What are these?" asked Adnan.

"Bills!" she shouted. "Bills! We will lose the house in ninety days! I married you because you were boring and responsible. Now you are poor and weird."

"Calm down, Naureen. I will take care of it," said Adnan. He was embarrassed that his wife had confronted him in front of all the members of the league. Money is an important part of family life. Being poor is like getting into a fight with a kung fu master and a wrestling champion at the same time. From one side, the kung fu master in his calm, swift manner is kicking your face because he can, and from the other side, the wrestling champion continues to bend and twist your body. But is this not the price of greatness?

Great men serve humanity at the cost of domestic bliss. What were the few bills compared to larger problems of the world? Sadly, Naureen did not understand this. She was a practical woman who wanted food for her children and shelter from the sky. Adnan wanted to look at the stars. He wanted to say to the world, "Here I am," and Naureen wanted to say, "Oh, there you are! Can you take the trash out?"

Naureen walked out of the room, not even allowing Adnan to explain himself. He stood at his desk, speechless. He picked up the bills, going through them only to avoid eye contact with the rest of us. The bills were from diverse backgrounds. Electricity provider, gas company, Internet, cable… it was an awkward moment.

"Forgive me, but I think we should leave," said Maaf Karna.

Hisaab Khan was more direct. "We should meet soon and talk about refinancing your mortgage," said Hisaab Khan in his useless manner, always relying on math to solve the problems of this world.

"I appreciate that," said Adnan in a soft voice that was more a result of his politeness than actual comprehension of how bad things were financially.

I had to pickup Adnan's mother from the mall, so I excused myself from the office and made my way to the driveway. Just as I started the car, I heard a knock on the window. It was Adnan.

"Do you mind if I join you? I don't want to be in the house right now."

It is a difficult thing to hang out with a man who has just fought with his wife, so I just kept my mouth shut. Throughout the trip Adnan remained silent and gloomy, making things even more awkward.

The mall is a dangerous place for a sad man. As we entered the mall two girls from a booth called *For Your Eyes Only* approached us. One of them said with a smile, "To get something good must we not suffer pain?"

"Yes" said Adnan. He felt he was connecting with them. "Yes, you are so right!"

Soon they had him sitting on a reclining chair much like that of a dentist. What he experienced next was more painful. Under a bright light the two girls used threads to pluck his eyebrows into shape. At every pluck of the hair, Adnan said, "ouch," "please stop," and "kill me now." But the girls continued pressing the thread hard against his eyebrows, trapping between the threads the small hair follicles of his brows and yanking them out of their natural home, his skin. After the procedure Adnan was crying. Not metaphorically but actual tears were falling from his eyes. The girls showed Adnan a mirror. I have to admit his eyebrows did look neater as if drawn by a pencil.

"You must get this done every month now," said the girl.

"I probably deserve it," said Adnan staring at his sad face in the mirror.

At the next booth a salesman in a silver shirt, black pants, and a snakeskin belt came toward us. His booth was called "*You Are the Pilot.*" The booth was full of tiny helicopters.

"I show you," he said in an accent that placed his origins somewhere in the castle of Dracula. Then, using a remote panel, he used his quick fingers to fly a small helicopter. We saw the small machine take off into the air. The clever salesman flew the helicopter around Adnan in circles all the while it was climbing higher, making Adnan dizzy.

"See how high it goes!" shouted the salesman. "From the floor it rises!"

This he demonstrated by flying the toy helicopter all the way up to the entrance of a department store on the second floor. And then putting the remote into the hands of Adnan, he said, "Fly my friend, fly! The next time you feel down, you can reach for your helicopter and reach new heights for only ninety-five dollars."

Adnan gave his credit card and became the owner of this most exciting device. He carried his new purchase in a large bag. "It's for Bubloo, not me."

But I could sense his weakness. We had barely walked farther when at the next booth a woman approached him. She was a chubby woman, wearing a long white dress with large orange sunflowers.

"Isn't life funny?" she asked like a best friend.

"You could say so," said Adnan. "Like a dark comedy."

"It can also get complicated, can it not?"

"Oh, believe me, it can," said Adnan.

"Yes, life has twists and turns," she said like an understanding schoolteacher. And then she asked Adnan the most tempting question.

"Would it not be amazing to just straighten everything out!"

"Yes!" said Adnan. "Oh yes."

In the next moment he was sitting on a chair and two women were performing a terrifying procedure, sandwiching his wavy hair between two hot irons. After doing this the woman held a mirror in front of his face. "All the curls and waves are gone. We straightened you out! Don't you love it?"

He didn't, but he still owed thirty-five dollars for the procedure. With locks of straightened hair falling in front of his thinned eyebrows, helicopter in hand, Adnan still looked sad. We bought some pretzels that tasted neutral. We were on our way to pick up his mother when he stopped to observe some mannequins in a display window.

For a few seconds Adnan froze like a statue. Looking at his thinned eyebrows and weirdly straight hair, I wondered if Adnan had lost the fight of life. Was he now ready to be spanked by society, and all the while say "thank you" for it? Had he become a generic, grocery-store cola with no personality? Just as I was pondering these questions, Adnan suddenly lifted his hands up in the air like a boxer after a winning fight, and shouted. "I GOT IT!"

Mission

"Adnan switched on the red light bulb and pulled the shower curtains close to emphasize the historical importance of this meeting"

H IS WORDS echoed throughout the mall and scared some people. A child nearby dropped his strawberry ice cream cone, and even the security guard became alert, grabbing the standard-issue flash light in his holster. Adnan's face had suddenly come back to life. Like an arcade machine that just received quarters he was ready to play the game of life.

"Minhaj! Let's find Mother quickly, we must go home. We have work to do!"

All the way to his mother, Adnan speed-walked, gliding between the many carts, ignoring their cries for attention. We found his mother and were soon on our way home. As we drove home, Adnan's mother wanted to discuss coupons, but Adnan was in his own world with the window rolled down, the wind hitting his silky, straightened hair.

At home he called an urgent meeting of the league, and in thirty minutes Hisaab Khan and Maaf Karna were sitting in the office. Adnan switched on the red light bulb and pulled the shower curtains closed to emphasize the historical importance of this meeting.

"Forgive me, but why have you called us here, and what have you done to your hair?" said Maaf Karna.

Hisaab was even less diplomatic. "You have barely three months before your house goes up for sale. And you are getting your eyebrows done?"

Adnan got up from his chair and placing the tips of his fingers on the desk, as was his habit, he explained.

"This morning I read that report in *Hi There News* about our great mission to Washington, DC. The press has been against me. My wife walked in and reminded me that our financial situation is desperate. I went to the mall..."

Here he stopped and turned around to look at the map of the world behind his desk. So far he had not said anything profound. He was describing his day and we found no inspiration in it.

He continued. "At the mall I was assaulted by the marketplace in the most painful manner. Look at these," he said, pointing to his well-shaped eyebrows.

"Yes, you look strange," said Hisaab Khan. And we all nodded in agreement.

Adnan made eye contact with each of us one by one as he said these words. "I then stared at mannequins, frozen statues that do not speak but simply resemble humans—just thinner, taller, and more stylish. I said to myself 'They would be better if they could speak.' And then my mind wandered, as it always does, to the future of things. I imagined a mannequin of the future that will speak and welcome curious customers into the store. You know...like an elegant robot."

"Forgive me, the idea is interesting, but I don't see your point."

"Exactly! There was no point to this mental wandering. And it is in these moments that the mind enters the playground of ideas. And then it struck me."

"Forgive me, but *what?*" Maaf Karna had lost his patience.

"The meaning, gentlemen! In ancient times men claimed to have spoken with animals, with rivers and trees, and were considered wise men. In our day our surroundings still speak to us."

"So what spoke to you? Tell us in five seconds," said Hisaab Khan.

Adnan smiled. We could see his teeth, part of his gums, he was so happy. "Everything! The whole day, the meeting we had, Naureen slamming the bills on this table, the mall, the highway upon which we drove."

"And what is everything telling you?" asked Hisaab Khan.

"We need to rent a moving truck."

"This is our last adventure with you"

"FORGIVE ME, but what will you do with the moving truck?"

"We are going to go door-to-door and collect used clothing. We shall continue this effort until the truck is full. Are you with me?"

"This is our last adventure with you," said Hisaab Khan. "We lived with a dangerous people, we witnessed the fall of men at a wedding, confronted a hateful senator, and—let's not forget—sat in the car with a man who set fire to a building."

Maaf Karna joined in. "Forgive me, but your wife spoke to me today. And we agree with her that you might be losing your mind."

"I am not losing! I am winning!" said Adnan. For the first time half of the league high command had combined against him. But soon he calmed himself down, as great men often do, demonstrating a self control needed at such times.

"I understand your feelings," said Adnan. "But do I have your loyalty for this last mission?"

Both Maaf Karna and Hisaab Khan agreed reluctantly.

The next morning we rented a fourteen-foot moving truck. Adnan had printed street maps for us. We divided into two teams. I went with Adnan. Maaf Karna and Hisaab Khan worked together, all the while grumbling and being negative about this community action. The whole day was spent going door-to-door asking for used clothing. Maaf Karna was getting the best response because he began his introduction with the words, "Forgive me for disturbing you...but do you have any used clothing to give us? We are collecting for someone with mental problems." In the first hour he had returned with several bags full of used clothing.

Hisaab Khan was also having success. He began his introduction by saying, "Experts believe that no one should own more than twenty items of clothing. More than that and it slows down your life. Perhaps you would like to get rid of some of the extra clothes that are slowing you down?"

With his approach, he returned with bags full of clothes and the truck was getting filled.

Adnan was also successful. I remember the first house we approached. I knocked on the door and we waited.

"I am nervous!" I said.

"Why? You used to deliver pizza. You should be comfortable with this."

"A pizza delivery man is the most welcome creature on earth. We are like Santa, and children never stop believing in us even after they become adults. They welcome us with loving eyes. This is not the same situation."

A woman answered the door. Her hair was tied in a towel and it seemed that we had disturbed her.

"Madam, we are collecting used clothing, would you have anything you would like to throw away?"

"My attic is full of old clothes. But what charity do you represent?"

"We just want your old clothes," said Adnan.

"I get it," she said. "First you do the eyebrows, then comes the women's clothing...it's a process, isn't it?"

Adnan kept silent. His feminine eyebrows were helping him complete his mission. She returned after twenty minutes with a box of clothes, and wished Adnan "good luck with your new life."

We learned it was easy to collect used things. Most were glad to get rid of them and some preferred to not answer the doorbell and just watch us from the inside while holding a cordless phone.

In the evening we returned to the house with our truck full of used clothing.

"Humanity is generous!" said Adnan. He invited us to eat with him. He had ordered pizza along with breadsticks, which went well with the garlic butter.

"Forgive me, but now our adventures have come to an end. We are glad you will donate these clothes to charity. It's always good to end a political career with an act of kindness," said Maaf Karna.

"End? No. It is just beginning!" said Adnan.

Hisaab Khan and Maaf Karna did not argue.

I was exhausted from all the work and fell upon the couch into the deep sleep that comes after eating pizza. In the middle of the night I heard a sound that woke me up. I saw Adnan leaving the house, attempting to close the door without making a sound. I was too tired to question him. I heard the truck starting, but then I fell asleep.

Reactions

"But how can something be found when we do not know what it looks like?"

<hr />

ARLY NEXT morning I woke up to the loud sounds of the morning news. I had been dreaming about delivering pizza to a colony of female astronauts on Jupiter. It was a wonderful dream that involved space travel, and I hate it when a good dream is broken by loud sounds of reality. From midnight till nine the couch, combined with the small table next to it, was considered my bedroom. Not in the traditional boring sense, because there were no walls to separate my space from the rest of the house. But an invisible wall existed between me and Adnan's family, kind of like the border between America and Canada. Friendly, invisible, and rarely respected. I kept my glacier-fresh body spray on the side table to symbolize my sovereignty over this area of the house. So I was upset to hear the loud sounds of the morning news with its silly introductory music.

"I'm sorry we wokc you up," said Naureen. "It's him." She was wearing her red silk dressing gown with Chinese style dragons embroidered on it. With morning laziness she lifted her coffee mug to point toward Adnan who sat on a chair in front of the TV with complete focus. He was already dressed

145

in a crisp white shirt and khakis. His hair was gelled and combed back neatly, but his eyes looked red.

"Minhaj, you woke up! I want you to see this."

I grabbed the leftover pizza from last night. I have to say that the people who came up with the concept of breakfast pizza really knew what they were talking about. When pizza is left out overnight, the tasty chemicals merge and create a subtle flavor. The cheese settles well into the tomato sauce and there is a chewiness to the whole experience that I find enjoyable. I sat next to Adnan and gave him a slice. He chewed on the pizza but kept his eyes on the TV, using the movement of his jaw to increase his focus.

Hi There News Traffic Report
I am bringing the most bizarre traffic news of my career. A portion of Highway 635 is a carpet. Yes, you heard me right. A carpet of clothes. Pants, shirts, skirts and shorts have been used to carpet the four lane highway. Here is a clip from our traffic helicopter.

The footage taken from a helicopter above Highway 635 showed clothing items lying on the highway. Cars and trucks drove over these clothes as they had probably done all night. I noticed Adnan had a smile on his face. Naureen laughed, shaking her head in disbelief.

"Who would be sick enough to do something like this? Spend hours putting clothes on the highway! That would take all night!"

Adnan looked at Naureen as he picked up the phone from the side table and dialed a number.

"Is this *Hi There News*? My name is Adnan Raheem Khan. I am responsible for dressing up Highway 635. I live in Dallas, Texas. Come to me."

Naureen glared at Adnan. It was the kind of look we give to a baby in a child seat at a Chinese restaurant who throws a hot spring roll into a glass of water. In her mind his madness was confirmed. Adnan did not seem apologetic. He behaved as if it was something very normal. He discussed the matter as one would discuss skim milk or whole-wheat bread. Without emotion.

"Trust me," he said getting up. "I am in control."

"You need professional help!" said Naureen. She ran into her room and in a few minutes came out dressed, holding her very large handbag, which was very expensive and an original something.

"Where are you going, Naureen?"

"Away from you!" It had to be the coffee shop. That is where female humanity goes in times of stress.

Another news flash appeared on the screen, featuring a mug shot of Adnan when he was arrested as the 635 bandit. The newscaster made the following announcement:

> *We have just received a phone call from a man who is claiming responsibility for the clothing items on Highway 635. He is Adnan Raheem Khan, also known as the '635 Bandit,' president of his own political party which comprises four members (him included). He has been arrested before for endangering the public and recently inflicted a food coma on a senator.*

Adnan turned to me and spoke in his calm methodical manner. "Get ready. Wear your best clothes. We are about to be famous." Since it was morning and that was something I did every day, I followed his instructions. I showered and got ready. When I came into the living room wearing my only tuxedo, Maaf Karna and Hisaab Khan were already there.

Hisaab Khan, who usually muttered his discontent under his breath, was today measurably upset. "On a scale of ten that measures my anger toward you, I am at nine point seven," he said, glaring at Adnan.

147

"Hisaab Khan, we seek greatness," continued Adnan. "But how can something be found when we do not know what it looks like?"

Other than Adnan, no one was in the mood for philosophy.

Maaf Karna was breathing heavily with anger and his voice oscillated between loud and shout. "Forgive me! Forgive me! You have broken the law and you are making absolutely no sense. And why is Minhaj wearing a tuxedo? Is this all some sick joke?"

"The feeling of commitment, gentlemen," continued Adnan. "When wanting something and having it are equally pleasurable, we call this state of being 'spiritual.' Indecision makes the spirit suffer. So the lesson is that if we do something, we must do it completely."

"Forgive me, but you are headed back to prison, where you can give these insane lectures."

"Let me ask you the most important question," said Adnan in his calm manner, which we now found very irritating. "Who among you wants to go to prison?"

"Forgive me, but never!"

"Not even for one second do I wish to be behind bars," said Hisaab Khan.

"I love my freedom!" I shouted.

"As do I," said Adnan. "According to my calculations based on the law enforcement shows, the police should arrive in ten minutes. Our only chance now is to go and pick up the clothes before the police arrests us."

"My feelings towards you are like a simultaneous equation," said Hisaab Khan. "A part of me wants to slap you and the other part wants to strangle you."

"There is no time for such violent behavior," said Adnan. "We must act as one. Minhaj, you will drive the truck as fast as you can toward the highway. I will ride with you in the front and Hisaab Khan and Maaf Karna will ride in the back of the truck."

We had no choice. The police would no doubt come looking for us. To express their anger, Hisaab Khan and Maaf
Karna squeezed in front with me and made Adnan sit in the
back of the truck. As we left the neighborhood I saw a van with
a satellite dish and antennas. It had *Hi There News* printed on
its side. I turned on the radio and every station was reporting
the same story.

> *Three men might be responsible for carpeting Highway
> 635 with clothing items. Wait, we have a call from someone.*
> *Caller: Yes, hello. Can you hear me? I am calling from a
> hot tub.*
> *Radio show host: Just barely. But please go on.*
> *Caller: Yesterday, a man visited my house. He asked for my
> used clothing. He was very non-threatening.*
> *Radio show host: how so?*
> *Caller: He asked for forgiveness before asking me for used
> clothing. I thought such a humble man deserves it. I gave
> him a large box full of used clothing. And this morning on
> the news I saw the helicopter footage. The camera zoomed in
> on one of these clothing items lying on the highway. I actually
> saw my old used jeans on TV!*

Maaf Karna had finally been recognized on national radio
for his politeness. He smashed his fist against the dashboard
many times, and each time he asked for forgiveness.

The *Hi There News* van which had just moments ago passed
us now appeared in the rearview mirror. They knew. I quickly
changed lanes, but so did the van. And behind this van were
other cars filled with cameramen and reporters. They were
all coming for us. One of the media cars came into the right
lane and their cameraman leaned out to take our picture.

"Are you members of the Desi League?" he shouted.

Maaf Karna tried to handle the situation. "Forgive me, but
we are in a hurry!"

"It is him! The apologist!" shouted the cameraman to the driver. "Slow them down! I can make the front page with these pictures and get enough money to make the mortgage this month!" They were not the only ones. In their eagerness to take our pictures they drove dangerously close and I had to slow down the truck.

"Soon the police will come for us," said Hisaab Khan. "And we will be arrested."

"Forgive me, but this is all Adnan's fault."

Their words were so empty of hope, so lacking in spirit like a soft drink that has lost all carbonation. Our leader, Adnan, was in the back of the truck.

Hisaab Khan was already making plans about life in prison. "I will write my second book on the beauty of fractions. We will have lots of time behind bars. Perhaps we could play mental math games. It will be a good learning experience for Minhaj."

The thought of being in prison with a math teacher who goes on and on about fractions terrified me. I realized that it was all up to me now. All those years in the fast-food business had trained me to react quickly. As a dishwasher at a pizza place, I had stunned the world of fast food with my dishwashing skills. Sanitizing, scrubbing, and drying the pans at a speed that others could only admire. I had been a successful delivery driver ready to sprint into action. When kids were hungry and mothers called for breadsticks it was I who had delivered. Outside a sandwich shop I had danced on the streets as a clown. Perhaps that was not relevant right now but it was a confidence booster.

"Hold on," I said grabbing the steering wheel tightly.

"Forgive me, but to what?"

"Yes, to what?" echoed Hisaab Khan like an angry twin.

"To each other," I said. I slammed the brakes. Both Hisaab Khan and Maaf Karna hit the windshield. I then heard a loud thump. It was Adnan bumping against the walls inside the truck.

"Forgive me, but do you want to kill us?"

There was no time to answer his tempting question. I had to focus. America is the New World, where people drive on the right-hand side of the road. But in Karachi where I had grown up, it is the opposite. We drive on the left side and once we start the car, we don't like to stop until we reach our destination. Things like stop signs, traffic lights—we consider these to be decorations, like a Christmas light or a disco ball at a party. We think they're pretty, but we never allow them to control our movement. We just keep going. In America, for the longest time I had continued my habit of driving on the left side, assuming that drivers coming from the opposite direction were drunk. I had paid a lot in fines. It had been expensive. And yet in doing these daring things I had learned a unique skill, which could not be written on a resume but now was our only hope.

I turned the steering wheel sharply and the truck lurched to the right. The media van shadowing us turned as well, barely avoiding collision. He honked angrily and both Hisaab Khan and Maaf Karna also screamed. I ignored everything and realized that there was not enough room on the road to make a U-turn. I pulled the gear into reverse and backed up to make more room. And then, putting the truck in drive, I stepped on the accelerator and charged toward oncoming traffic.

Hisaab Khan and Maaf Karna shouted like children riding a rough roller coaster. Children who know bad words. I dodged oncoming traffic by staying in the center lane. Most of the cars swerved left or right, missing us by inches. My real challenge was the *Hi There News* van. It was filled with reporters and a photographer who had been leaning outside to take pictures of our truck. As I headed straight toward this van, the photographer quickly moved in and put on his seat belt.

"We are all going to die," wailed Hisaab Khan. "The probability of living through this is very low!"

We were now on a collision course. The van driver was not turning away, and I was heading right toward them. I kept my foot on the accelerator, because any sign of slowing down would betray weakness. I could see the eyeballs of the driver. For a moment we locked eyes and I wondered, "Is he nuts?"

He turned out to be normal and shouted something obscene as he turned to the right at the last moment. The van hit our side mirror breaking the brittle plastic and crunching the glass like cereal. Our truck shook as the van scraped against our passenger door and the side of the truck. Maaf Karna saw the van very closely from his passenger seat and made his peace with God by screaming his confessions.

We survived. The cars ahead of us moved out of the way which gave me enough time to take a quick exit onto a nearby street. We were free.

Maaf Karna and Hisaab Khan expressed their complaints against me in language that is not appropriate for children under ninety.

Pickup

"The officer looked at Adnan and kept his hands on his belt which held a gun, a flashlight, and scary-looking handcuffs"

"D

O YOU realize that more than 30,000 people die in traffic accidents every year? How dare you challenge probability!"

"Forgive me, but once we stop this truck I will slap you silly."

Their angry words soon blended into words of advice. "Take a left, take a right, go here, go there..."

In just minutes we had reached the part of Highway 635, which Adnan, the president of our Desi League, had carpeted with used clothing. A number of cop cars were parked on the shoulder of the highway. I parked behind them and quickly ran to open the door to the back of the truck. Adnan was on the floor of the truck like a gecko, using his palms to somehow grab the floor.

"Gentlemen, I now know what a racquet ball feels like."

"Forgive me, but there is no time to discuss sports," said Maaf Karna. "You must talk to the police and allow us to get those clothes off the highway."

"We have risked our lives to get you here on time," said Hisaab Khan, as if it had all been done by him.

Adnan tucked his shirt back into his pants and ran his fingers through his hair to make it neat again. We followed him as he approached a police officer who was parked at the shoulder of the highway. Thanks to *Hi There News*, Adnan was already famous and the police officer recognized him. The officer looked at Adnan and kept his hands on his belt, which held a gun, a flashlight and scary-looking handcuffs.

"Sir, did you do this?"

"Yes, officer. I am responsible for this."

"You have quite a wardrobe, sir," said the officer.

"I like choices," said Adnan.

At this reply the officer smiled but then suppressed the joy that comes with laughter, because he wanted to appear professional in front of the many cameras watching his every move. "You do realize that there is going to be a fine for this," he said. "This is not an accident. These clothes did not fall out of your truck. You have carefully placed the clothes next to each other like you were making a collage or a quilt. In some places you have placed shirts over a pair of jeans and below the jeans there are socks almost like a two dimensional scarecrow moon-bathing on a highway."

"Yes, it was time-consuming, matching all the pants with the right shirt, but my wife has trained me well," said Adnan.

"Sir, you are artistic. I'll give you that. You can do all the arts and crafts inside your home. But this is the highway. Your behavior is against the law."

Adnan nodded in agreement and we were grateful that he did not argue. "I wish to correct this problem, officer, by picking up all these clothes."

"That would be helpful," said the officer. He then walked over to some other cops for a discussion. One of them took out an orange cone from a police car and placed it on the road. They had taken Adnan's suggestion. They were blocking Highway 635. Soon all incoming traffic was blocked and the reporters were taking pictures from the roofs of their vehicles. The police officer came back to Adnan.

"Okay sir, pick it all up."

Thrilled that we were not going to jail we sprang into action. It was an odd feeling, running around on the broad, always-busy Highway 635 at ten in the morning as if it were a playground. The cameras captured our every move as we picked up the clothes and put them into bags the cops had given us.

Adnan seemed happy about this. For the next hour, we ran all over the blocked highway picking up these dirty clothes. The helicopter belonging to *Hi There News* hovered above us reporting live. Adnan waved a pair of jeans at the helicopter as if he were stranded on some island.

We picked up all the clothes, and the truck was once again filled with bags of clothing. As Adnan did paper work with the police officer, we waited for him in the truck. Hisaab Khan had taken the wheel and refused to let me drive.

As soon as he was done, Adnan walked over and congratulated us. "Well done! This is a great victory for the League. Now go home; I will join you there!"

"Where are you going?" I asked.

Adnan had already joined the reporters in the stalled traffic. Among them was the *Hi There News* van we had almost crashed into. "Do you not wonder why I did all this?"

"Oh yes!" shouted the reporters. "We are most curious!"

"Please tell us!" shouted another reporter from the roof of an SUV. "I want to understand how your mind works. I care about you."

"I will buy you an extra-large soda if you tell us," cried out another journalist.

"Very well," said Adnan. "Give me a ride back to my house and there I will reveal everything." *Hi There News,* which had once been his enemy, now welcomed Adnan into their van. They turned on the air conditioner at high speed for him. We followed them back to Adnan's house in a procession of cars, vans, and trucks to the sounds of the news helicopter hovering above us.

"This made them hyper, and some were doing pushups"

———◆———

WHEN WE reached the house, it was like a royal wedding minus the inherited wealth, outdated costumes, and funny hats. Photographers ran here and there, taking up positions with their cameras. The journalists wore baseball caps, ate energy bars, and drank strong coffee. This made them hyper, and some were doing pushups.

They had no better news item to report. Even though some scientists had made breakthroughs in the field of medical research, the journalists did not feel that those things were worthy for television. In any case, medical discoveries are complicated things with long and difficult names. To be on the news it is important to always make the viewer feel, *Oh no, he didn't!* Humanity loves to feel this.

Adnan arrived in the *Hi There News* van like a head of state. As he got out of the car, photographers were stepping on one another's toes shouting questions.

Ignoring all of them Adnan walked over to us. "Gentlemen, let's get these bags of clothes out of the truck!"

Hisaab Khan and Maaf Karna stood aside in silence, doing nothing, to express their anger. I joined Adnan in unloading the bags. As I was dragging a bag of clothes inside the house, Adnan said, "No! Just empty the bags right here in the front yard."

"What?"

"Just empty the clothes right here," he said. "Yes, here."

He demonstrated by emptying a bag on the grass on the front yard.

Maaf Karna could not control himself and came out of ignore mode. "Forgive me, but what are you doing?"

"Something good," said Adnan.

The media was once again snapping pictures and reporting these strange actions. They loved it when things got crazy.

"Minhaj, let's do this," said Adnan. "Empty the bags right here!"

"Don't you do it, Minhaj," said Hisaab Khan. "I am going to say it only once!"

"Forgive me, but if you have any respect for me and Hisaab Khan you will not listen to Adnan," said Maaf Karna sternly.

I immediately helped Adnan empty all the bags one by one on the front yard. We kept doing this until the thousands of clothes became a hill reaching about as high as the roof of the house.

Then Adnan did something shocking. He turned toward this mountain of clothing and shouted with a voice full of anger. "You silly fabrics! You were picked up from the road, and no one cares about you! Oh you rejected shirts, you have holes and stains and oil marks all over you. All you pathetic pants, you disgust me! You silly, frilly skirts, you crazy scarves, you are without hope! No one cares about you!"

Even I was convinced that Adnan had gone crazy. The reporters, already very excited due to the drinking of strong coffee, were shouting their questions. Meanwhile Adnan kept yelling at this hill of clothing. I became worried about the great leader. If there was one thing about his nature, it was that he always remained polite. His angry words and insulting behavior toward the clothes was something new and out of his nature.

"Forgive me, but he has now lost it," said Maaf Karna. "How simple and good was his life only a few months ago. This is what happens to a man when he tries to become some kind of leader."

"He is now scoring zero on the 'barely normal' scale," said Hisaab Khan.

Adnan turned toward me and spoke in a whisper. "I want you to do what I am doing. Pull all the anger you feel from your past and take it out on these clothes. Just let them have it."

Anger was always a few memories away. I thought about my math teachers and their sarcastic comments. How they had introduced me to negative numbers by giving me minus three out of ten. I remembered cheating in chemistry class from a boy who knew even less than me but had seemed intelligent because he wore glasses. I remembered all the men who had appeared in Hawaiian shirts in late night infomercials promising me a rich lifestyle for three easy payments of thirty-nine ninety-nine.

Taking these feelings, I found a shirt inside this mountain of clothes and made it my enemy.

"Oh, you think you are so clever! Give me back my money! Give me back those nights!" I charged toward a colorful shirt that looked Hawaiian and punched it. I body slammed a few scarves and landed my elbow on a pair of black jeans.

I got so carried away that Adnan caught hold of me. "I think that is enough."

I was breathing anger and it took me a few moments to calm down. I lay on the ground looking at the sky, wiping the angry tears that had come to my eyes. Adnan was calm now. He walked over to the cameramen and reporters, who waited for his words in complete silence.

Then one of them, a veteran news media personality who had interviewed presidents, kings, and queens burst out with curiosity. "Mr. Adnan, why do you do this? Why did you insult these clothes?"

They all went silent waiting for Adnan's answer. Hisaab Khan and Maaf Karna paused where they were standing. Even a chipmunk that had been eating an acorn put it aside and looked at Adnan.

Adnan took a deep breath and spoke loudly. "Ladies and gentlemen, these clothes are now for sale."

All the reporters burst out laughing.

The famous journalist gave his opinion in an arrogant pompous voice. "Surely you are joking! Who on earth wants to buy wrinkled clothes with holes, oil marks, tire stains, mud, and are torn to shreds!"

All this was live on TV. These words were heard by celebrities, fashion designers, and most important, the teenagers. Among the teenagers of the world there was extra excitement. All year they spent their time at the mall looking for expensive jeans that were torn at the knees, or shirts that were torn on the sleeve. And so the teenagers, in their own quick manner, using words that only they understood, sent text messages to one another by the thousands.

"OH MY GOD, OMG, OMG. There is a sale on distressed jeans and clothes!"

Adnan now made the speech that he had prepared for the media. "Ladies and gentlemen, in the mall you find jeans that have holes in them and are torn at the knees. We have gone a step further. These clothes are stained with oil and mud, and some even have remains of animals on them. I have also taken the time to personally abuse these items. So among our collection you will find distressed jeans, harassed shirts, abused jackets, and shirts that began their career as full sleeve now made sleeveless by rough treatment. And one more thing," he said raising his forefinger to the sky so the helicopter above could see him.

"Unlike other designer clothes these clothes were made this way in America by Americans. Because all night they drove over these." Adnan had used the assembled press to send his message loud and clear.

He turned toward us and addressed us, the members of the Desi League. "Organize, gentlemen! You are to be cashiers and sell each item for no less than five hundred dollars."

"Forgive me, but that is an insane price! These clothes are damaged!"

"Exactly," said Adnan. "Follow me now."

We followed him into the house. He instructed us to pick up the dining table and three chairs and place these outside in the front yard. Soon we were outside setting this table in front of the mountain of clothing. This would serve as our checkout counter. Maaf Karna, Hisaab Khan, and I took our seats at this table facing the street. We were now three cashiers waiting for customers. I felt like a celebrity in my tuxedo, with so many photographers taking my picture.

"Forgive me, but this is really silly. How long are we supposed to wait here?"

Maaf Karna's question was answered by the loud sounds of teenagers arriving. They came on skate boards, cycles, cars, and some even walked. The teenagers are a huge community and the elite among them are known as the cool crowd. They came with their ruffled hair and lifted collars. The famous reporter who had criticized Adnan for announcing the sale now interviewed a teenager.

"Why have you come here?"

"To buy these fly clothes. Why else?" said the teenager.

"But why these clothes?"

"In the mornings before school we spend a lot of time trying to look casual. We work hard to appear as if we are not trying. As you can see, my hair is all ruffled up as if my head was in a tornado. I spent thirty minutes creating this," he said pointing to his hair which was a magnificent mess. "With this look I can be part of the cool, carefree crowd. Now if I can get these clothes I can go a step further and be part of the *just-been-in-an-accident* crowd."

"When did the *just-been-in-an-accident crowd* become cool?" asked the journalist.

"Five minutes ago when you asked on television who would buy these clothes. You see, we teenagers think you're a big square. And if you don't like something, then for us it becomes the coolest thing on earth."

While the teenagers were digging through the mountain of clothing, a famous film star arrived in a limousine. He had his reasons to be here.

"As a celebrity I live in a bubble of luxury. I walk on a plush red carpet and people clap for me. And that's when I am working! So I live a life of safe luxury. By wearing these roughed-up clothes I will feel down-to-earth as if I am part of the normal world experiencing challenges in life. It's either this or actually getting a real job. And who wants that?"

Speculators who made their living investing in all kinds of markets also arrived. When asked why he was buying such rough, destroyed clothing one of them said, "If I can get these clothes I can probably repackage them and sell them to somebody else, who will think that he can sell them to somebody else for a higher price. I love making money from such bubbles!"

Such investors drove the price up and the price of a shirt was now thirty thousand dollars. In just a few hours the hill of clothes had been reduced to a small pile. We had sold thousands of items to cool teenagers, celebrities, and speculators.

With just one shirt and a pair of shorts remaining, Adnan told us to stop the sale. He approached one of the cameras and announced, "These last two clothing items will be auctioned to the highest bidder."

We were approached by a representative from a museum of history. He made a bid for the shirt. "These clothes represent an event in America. That's what history is. We must display these clothes in our museum. There is story behind them. We are willing to pay six million for those shorts."

We happily took a check from them. Moments later we were approached by a representative from another museum. She made the winning bid for the last remaining shirt, which was torn so badly that only the collar was intact. "We want to enter the auction because we come from the Museum of Irony. These clothes are fetching millions of dollars as some kind of American product. Yet if we look at the labels, we can see that most of these clothes are manufactured in China, and most of the cars that drove over them were Japanese and run on Arabian oil. The irony itself is inescapable. We will pay eight million for the shirt."

"They think of higher things like global warming and asteroids"

A FTER THIS great yard sale, the many reporters who had been so excited left Adnan's house. They were sad at the happy ending. They also felt used, which was something new for them. We pulled bags of cash into the living room. Adnan collapsed on the couch and fell asleep. We did not disturb the great man and spoke in happy whispers.

Naureen returned to the house with a very large cup of cold chocolate drink. She was upset about the mess she saw in the front yard. "What happened today?" she asked. "I saw cups of coffee in the front yard and the grass is messed up."

"We held a successful yard sale," I said.

"Whatever," she said looking at Adnan, who was now in deep sleep on the couch. "Tell him to stay there." She walked into her room and slammed the door shut.

We counted the money till late hours of the night with Hisaab Khan making exact thousand-dollar bundles, and Maaf Karna adding rubber bands around these bundles of cash.

The next morning both Maaf Karna and Hisaab Khan returned. It was really nice of them, because Adnan had not even called a meeting. And yet here was Hisaab Khan holding cups of fresh coffee in a carrying box, and Maaf Karna had with him a box of freshly baked doughnuts. I love surprise breakfasts! If countries did that for each other, there would be no war. The fragrance of sugary doughnuts was in the air. It combined well with the aroma of the hot, creamy coffee and awakened Adnan.

"What a day we had yesterday, gentlemen!" he said, rubbing his eyes. Then he saw the bundles of cash that we had placed neatly on the living-room floor. I had slept on them as Adnan had taken the couch.

"How much is that?" he asked.

"Sixteen million dollars," I said barely believing it myself. It was weird. I had never spoken so much money before, let alone counted it. Adnan held his natural dignity and formal demeanor. He got up from the couch, tucked his shirt in, and fixed his hair. He looked serious, because for great men money is not everything. They think of higher things, like global warming and asteroids. He did, however, roll on the floor from one end of the living room to the other, kicking the air as if riding an imaginary cycle. After this, we gathered in his office and ate the doughnuts of victory in silent joy.

Adnan broke the silence with even greater news. "We will split the money equally among all members of the league."

Maaf Karna lost control of his happiness. "Forgive me," he said jumping from his chair, "but I must kiss you."

Even before Adnan could object to this horror, Maaf Karna planted his lips on the forehead of Adnan.

Hisaab Khan grabbed Adnan's hand and shook it wildly. "That comes to four million for each of us," he said. "There will be taxes and other issues, I am sure."

I could not care less about such technical details and was unable to control my excitement. "I am getting a helicopter!"

Naturally Maaf Karna felt that it was his duty to bring me down. "Forgive me, but you should not waste all your wealth on something so silly."

"Yes, spend wisely," added Hisaab Khan. "You should get an education because, frankly, you are very innocent—and not in a good way."

The next few days we spent dividing the money and opening our bank accounts. It was a big change for me. I usually kept my money in an empty jam jar. It both scented my cash with strawberry and was fairly secure. But now that we had millions, our wealth required formal storage. The helpful people at the bank came to our rescue and were so nice to us that I wondered why some people are angry at them. They gave us iced lemonade; the manager said that he loved us all like family.

It was time for me to move out. I booked a room at a hotel where I would be living temporarily in luxury, watching TV, bathing under pressurized water, and using too many towels to dry myself. Adnan's house had been good to me. I said goodbye to the couch on which I had slept. I bade farewell to his office where behind the shower curtain the great leader had expressed his thoughts.

Before I left, Adnan called me to his office. "I want to present you with a medal of honor," he said. And then from his desk he took out a sock. It was from the day we had spent with the tribe of Missisoka. Using a safety pin, he attached the beautiful yellow-and-blue striped sock to my front pocket. I saluted him.

"Truly" he said, "we have hunted well."

College

"Such comparisons filled me with wonder"

L IVING IN the hotel was like being in paradise. Now I knew why men run after money: so they can live in hotels. In my room, I slept on a giant bed with fresh bedsheets changed regularly by nice people in uniforms. I spent many days just watching TV, learning about the world from important shows that discussed who needed a makeover. Nearby was a community college and this institution would open my eyes—every day, because the first class was at nine a.m.

At the community college, I introduced myself to all the teachers as a seeker of wisdom. The physics teacher gave me a very high compliment. After listening to my views about the world, he said, "Your knowledge of this world is an atom." I was flattered because the professor greatly admired the atom and other small things.

"Today," he said to our class, "I am going to discuss with you the amazing world of nano."

"I object," I said loudly. "I signed up for physics, and while I am sure your grandmother is a great lady, we do not have time for family stories."

The professor ignored my objection and picked up the apple that I had given him at the beginning of the class. "Nanoparticles are very small. So small that this apple is about as much bigger than a nanoparticle as the earth is bigger than this apple."

I could not believe that things so small even existed! If we ate apples, which were to nanoparticles the size of the earth, then what were we? Giants who ate worlds and baked them into pies? Such comparisons filled me with wonder. I wondered what had gone wrong with my schooling in Pakistan. In school the teachers had never raised the excitement level even to medium. Our aim in life was to arrive at answers that were already present at the back of our textbooks. Where there was no mystery, how could we be curious? Our highest aspiration had been to exist as obedient copycats and copydogs. And so we had escaped from such labor to other things such as flying paper planes and thumb wrestling, at which I had become quite good.

One day, Hisaab Khan called me and asked me to meet him and Maaf Karna at a nearby restaurant. While I did not miss them, I decided that a quick lunch with them should not be too painful. We met at the restaurant and ordered miniburgers, which looked beautiful, like small, doll versions of the real thing.

Maaf Karna seemed anxious, and finally he spoke about what was bothering him. "Forgive me, but we are meeting today for an important reason. Naureen called me three days ago from Florida," he said, dipping a fry into a small puddle of ketchup on his plate.

"I love ketchup," I said. "Wherever you go there is ketchup. In the desert inside a tent or on a mountain in Switzerland. It's there! Everyone needs it."

"Pay attention for one minute, if you can," said Hisaab Khan. "This is serious. Naureen thinks Adnan is wasting all his money on an insane project."

I felt I had to defend Adnan, who had been a great leader to us all.

"You just don't get it, do you? Adnan is probably involved in some kind of charity work. He has a higher vision. But how would you know of these things? You have not studied geology. You don't know about the Pangaea. Do you know that we are moving through space right now around the sun at more than fifty thousand miles per hour?"

"Forgive me, but you have barely spent two months in college, and you are lecturing us?"

"Just show it to him," said Hisaab Khan, "before he starts talking about mayonnaise, mustard and other nonsense."

Maaf Karna reached into his pocket, pulled out a newspaper and placed it next to the cheeseburgers.

HI THERE NEWS

Eccentric millionaire Adnan Raheem Khan, the man responsible for drugging a United States senator, destroying twenty-five percent of a dollar store, and documented fabric abuser is now involved in a bizarre project on the coastline of Florida. Using his new wealth he has purchased two aircraft carriers and one antique ship. He had these combined into one massive ship which he calls the "ARK." These are also the initials of his name. This brings the megalomania of this man to a new level.

171

"Even with all his money Adnan remained employed by his inner voice"

———

"**F**ORGIVE ME, but this man," said Maaf Karna, pointing to the newspaper, "has made us wealthy. We must go and save him from his stupidity."

It was difficult to argue with that. Instead of going to the mall and buying clothes like decent people and feeling happy in the food court, Adnan was spending his money on aircraft carriers. A few burgers and fries later, we decided to go immediately to Florida, to prevent him from "future madness" as Maaf Karna put it. Outside the restaurant in the parking lot, Maaf Karna pointed to a pearl-white muscle car. It had vanity number plates: *4GIV*. As soon as we sat inside this German machine, I was impressed by the soft but firm manner in which the doors closed, sealing us from the outside world inside an air-conditioned cabin filled with the fragrance of newness.

We reached the airport and took the earliest flight to Florida. I was grateful that this time I got to sit inside the plane. Throughout the flight, Hisaab Khan kept asking me to provide him with "any two numbers. Just any two numbers, any two..." He wanted to add them or multiply them in his sick mind without using a calculator. I changed seats and spent the rest of the flight wondering about Adnan. What was he up to? Why an aircraft carrier? Why not a hot-air balloon?

We landed in sunny Florida and I was impressed by the airport. The airport offered neck and shoulder massage but sadly there was no time for it. We rented a silver convertible and sped toward the coastline. Naureen had provided Maaf Karna with the address and we reached it in less than an hour.

The shipping dock was busy with activity, but Adnan was not difficult to find. He stood on an elevated platform in front of the most massive ship we had ever seen. Only the side of the ship was visible, and to us it appeared as an unending wall of gray steel. The word ARK was painted on it in red; each letter was the size of a small house. This great ship cast a shadow on Adnan and the reporters he was addressing. They all looked tiny in front of it. Adnan was wearing his usual khakis, crisp white shirt, and navy blue jacket but also, on his head was a captain's hat.

"Ladies and gentlemen," he spoke into a microphone and pointed to the massive ship behind him, "This is not just a large ship. It is a way of life." Even with all his money, Adnan remained employed by his inner voice. He listened to the beating of his heart and not the beating that society had given him or the one he had received in prison.

The reporters still remained hostile to Adnan. One of the reporters who had been present at the great yard sale asked angry questions. "Mr. Adnan, why have you spent all your wealth on these aircraft carriers?"

Adnan loved the word 'why' more than anyone and responded with another question. "Why did Van Gogh paint?"

"Because he was good at it," said the reporter, making a lot of sense.

But this only added more enthusiasm to Adnan's voice. "Exactly! This is my canvas. What you see behind me is the ARK of the Desis. It was constructed by joining two antique aircraft carriers and one ancient wooden ship from Norway.

On this ARK we will go on a journey of self-discovery, breathe fresh air, and bite into oranges without peeling them."

"But why don't you just go to West Virginia? They have trees and nature," asked one silly reporter who was not grabbing the vision.

"The Desis must confront nature. Their creative spirit can only be unleashed when the need to survive has completely overwhelmed them. It is only then that useless rituals are rejected and reason prevails. I call all Desis to come and join me on this ARK, on which we will sail away."

"Your estimated wealth was four million dollars after that yard sale. How did you manage to buy and join two aircraft carriers?"

"There are no aircraft on this ship," said Adnan. "So that made it affordable. I received a further discount because the ARK carries no fuel."

"Following his dreams had made him stronger"

————◆————

THIS INVITED great laughter from all the reporters. A journalist from *Hi There News* gave his judgment with a victorious smile. "Surely, Mr. Khan, you have been most silly with your money! A ship without fuel is not going anywhere!" The reporters agreed with mocking laughter, and it was on this note that the press conference ended.

We caught up with Adnan as he wandered slowly, lost in thought in the great shadow of his ARK. Hisaab Khan tapped him on the shoulder but Adnan mistook his hand for a journalist.

"Sorry, I have no further comments," he said without looking back.

"Forgive me, but we do."

Hearing the familiar voice of apology Adnan turned around with a smile. The discouragements from the press had probably gotten him down. He must have felt the need to be among friends who would discourage him in a more familiar manner. He greeted us enthusiastically shaking our hands with a firm grip.

"The League is back!"

Maaf Karna pointed to the massive mountain of a ship parked in the water and said, "Forgive me, but we are not here to join you in your madness."

Hisaab Khan added his own comments. "You must stop this ARK nonsense. You have spent more than eighty percent of your wealth on this extravagance."

I did not want to verbally agree with Hisaab Khan and Maaf Karna, but in this case they were right. I nodded in agreement.

Adnan stood there listening to our practical advice. In his captain's hat and navy jacket he looked ready for adventure, like a child who happily gets ready for a day at the beach with his bucket and spade, and anticipates building a sand castle. And yet he was a grown man who shaved his jaw with menthol-enhanced shaving cream. He had a wife and two lively children who liked to watch television at all times. He needed to act like an adult and discuss how much money he had lost in stock market, play golf, and redesign his patio. But those were normal things. And this was Adnan Raheem Khan.

In his typical manner, he ignored our concerns and invited us into his life. "Let me show you the ARK. It is truly amazing!"

We followed him, walking in the shadow of the ARK to the bridge, which inclined steeply, like a staircase leading to the high entrance of this massive ship. We used the railing to pull ourselves forward. Beneath us water ripples broke against the massive hull. While Maaf and Hisaab were breathing heavily, exhausted by the climb, Adnan barely used the railing and was walking upward with considerable ease. Following his dreams had made him stronger.

"When we leave land for water," he said in his usual philosophical manner, turning his face upward, "we feel we have left our natural environment. But gentlemen, 70 percent of the earth is water. Are we not coming home?"

"Forgive me," said Maaf Karna, breathing heavily. "You have achieved this at a great cost. And how high is this ship? I feel as if I am climbing a mountain."

"That is the idea," said Adnan patting Maaf Karna on the shoulder. "I had the ship built in a way that the deck is very high. I want to exist on a higher plane."

We finally crossed the bridge and entered the ARK. Standing on it was very similar to being on a roller coaster that pauses for a second at its highest peak and gives us a panoramic view of everything below. Things that overwhelm and obstruct seemed tiny and insignificant from here. It was more than just a ship or a vessel or some machine of transport. This was a land in the sky. The metallic deck beneath our feet stretched like a six-lane highway all the way to the other end, where the great big anchor for this massive ship appeared as a small toy.

From one side we could see the docks below us and beyond that the world of normal with its clusters of buildings and snaking highways. The other side of the ARK faced the ocean, which spread out like a sheet of shimmering blue silk.

"In the mornings I go jogging," said Adnan. "One lap of this Ark is two miles. The fresh sea air does good things for me."

Just near the entrance was a bright-yellow-colored utility vehicle with no roof or windshield, like something we see in airport terminals. He sat in the driver's seat, and Maaf Karna joined him in the front. Hisaab Khan and I took the back seats as Adnan turned on the engine, which sounded like a hand dryer in a sophisticated restroom. It moved smoothly on the metal deck, the sea breeze hitting our faces as we took in the majestic view. There is something about the sea. It does increase our happiness by 70 percent.

He stopped to show us the great metal scar where the two aircraft carriers had been joined. He drove farther and surface of the ship merged into planks of wood. "This is the third ship that was used to create the ARK," he explained.

"Forgive me, but how old was that ship?"

"It was owned by Vikings. They are now dead but one of their descendents was selling the ship online. While he is proud of his ancestry, he now wants to get into the frozen yogurt business. So he needed some start-up capital. I only paid a million for it—I felt like a pirate! But can you feel it, gentlemen? The spirit of the Vikings? The courage of warriors?"

"Forgive me, but I feel nothing," said Maaf Karna. But as he said this, his hair was blowing in the wind, and I could see that he sat very comfortably. After this brief tour Adnan drove us to the only structure that interrupted the flat surface of this ARK. It was a blue-colored building about seven stories high that held on its roof a large circular room with walls of glass.

"That used to be the control tower. It was from that building that planes were guided for takeoff and landing."

"Forgive me, but how is it useful to you?"

"I live in it."

He parked outside the building just as normally as a person parks his car outside a house. As we approached the building, the front door automatically slid open and we entered a large room with a marble floor. The walls were covered with the paintings of Adnan's illustrious ancestors. Just below a large oil painting of Cellular Khan, there was a green leather sofa and a lamp. Soft neutral music filled the air as Adnan pushed a button on the wall. We were going up.

"Gentlemen, I love elevators. They are uplifting. But they make them so small! Here I have enlarged it into a comfortable room."

Maaf Karna, who was sitting on the green leather sofa, expressed his objection.

"Forgive me, this wastage of money is an insanity. But this sofa is very comfortable."

The elevator opened into the brightest room I have ever seen. It was a large circular room covered with thick white carpet with a circular wall of glass. There was so much light that Adnan put on his sunglasses. I saw Tina practicing yoga on a mat while she stared out at the ocean, Bubloo was watching a movie about dinosaurs on a flat-screen television. Adnan's mother was sitting at a dining table studying a catalog with the latest comforters. Naureen reclined on a couch, reading a book titled *How to Deal with a Madman*. When she saw us, she put the book down and jumped up to meet us.

"Thank you so much for coming here!"

Adnan was puzzled. "Oh, you called them here?"

"Yes I did," said Naureen. "I need their help to convince you that all this is crazy."

"But you said you wanted a bigger house!" said Adnan.

Naureen ignored Adnan and spoke to us. "I was so excited when he said he had bought us a new home. He said it was a surprise, so I allowed him to blindfold me all the way from the airport. After a long journey of walking and climbing, I finally opened my eyes on this crazy ship. Now you tell me: Is he mad, or am I mad for being here?"

Maaf Karna nodded in agreement. "Forgive me, but I think your husband is the president of madness."

"Imagine my children growing up on an aircraft carrier. No neighbors, no children to play with. No walking to the nearby grocery store or discussing life with the family next door?"

"But you never did those things anyway," said Adnan.

"I want to now," said Naureen, raising her voice to an emotional level. "Where are the people? Normal families need people!"

"I have already invited the Desis to come and join us on this ARK," said Adnan. "The ARK can easily hold twenty thousand people. Bubloo and Tina will have many friends."

"Forgive me, but no one will join you here on this ship."

But giving up was not in Adnan's nature. "I have an appointment tomorrow with a leading family among the Desis. If they decide to move to the ARK, others are sure to follow. As members of the league, you must join me on this mission."

"*We are so compatible*"

I N THE morning we sat at a table on the deck of the ARK, eating a good breakfast. Naureen had made omelets and pancakes. She was grateful for our presence and hoped that perhaps we could convince Adnan to give up his ARK project. Adnan was wearing his captain's hat along with his signature crisp white shirt, khakis, and navy-blue jacket. Tina was doing cartwheels in a ballet costume, and Bubloo was flying a kite. The fresh air had made them more active. Adnan carefully coated toast with cream cheese as he briefed us on our diplomatic mission.

"Now let me give you a little background on DC Khan. His complete name is Double Click Khan. Even in intellectual circles he is known as a square. You might find that he is a bit different, but he is important, and it will be a huge victory for the cause if he can join us on the ARK."

After breakfast we drove to DC Khan's house, which was located in a pleasant neighborhood of orderly trees and well-trimmed front yards. We rang the bell, and a chubby man of medium height with round glasses opened the door. He wore loose jeans and a denim shirt with a company logo embroidered on its pocket. He was expecting us.

"You must be Adnan. Please come in."

"Very nice to meet you Double Click," said Adnan.

"Please, no need to be formal. Just call me Click," he said shaking our hands as we entered his living room. We took our seats on the sofa and Double Click sat in a comfortable computer chair facing us.

"So what brings you to my home?"

There was no small talk in him.

"You must have heard about our most recent campaign in Washington, DC."

"I read about that on the *Hi There News* website. You ate kebabs in Washington, DC, with a senator. And now you are building a ship."

"Not just a ship," said Adnan, "We are building a new society. We want you to join us."

Double Click paused to consider the request by looking at the floor. "I can join you by video chat..."

"I would like you to join us in person," said Adnan "We would like you to be there. Your presence will boost everyone's confidence."

"Let me get you some drinks," said Double Click. Just as he returned with glasses filled with cold orange soda, a small boy of about twelve came running into the room. He spoke a strange language.

"Zero one one zero zero."

"English, English! We have guests," said Double Click.

Double Click placed his hand on the boy's shoulders.

"This is my son, Mouse."

"Hello, Mouse, how do you do?" asked Adnan. Why would anyone call their son Mouse? In fact people, when keeping animal names, usually went for more majestic animals like lion, eagle, monkey, or baboon. But Mouse? Who does that? We were enjoying the orange soda when a young girl entered the living room. She looked a year younger than Mouse. Double Click gestured toward her.

"This is my daughter, Keyboard."

"Nice to meet you, Keyboard," said Adnan shaking her hand and patting her on the head.

And then Maaf Karna, who could never control himself in these situations, asked the question on all our minds. "Forgive me, but are these the real names of your children?"

"Yes of course," said Double Click with a smile.

There was silence in the room. Mouse was crouching on the floor and crawling at a very high speed. Keyboard was performing a strange dance as if some imaginary large finger was poking her all over her body. Then a woman entered the living room. She was dressed in casual long shirt and pants. Finally, I thought, here is someone more normal.

Double Click introduced her. "This is my wife. She is the Monitor."

At this we all laughed, because we thought he was joking. But Double Click and his wife did not join us in our laughter, which embarrassed us. His wife, Monitor, was still nice to us.

"Would you all like to stay for lunch?"

We agreed and soon we joined them at the table. The children had changed their clothes for lunch. Mouse wore a T-shirt that said in bold letters, "*Byte me.*" Keyboard was wearing a sweat shirt that summarized her view of life: "*Delete or be deleted*".

After the usual discussion about the weather, the Weather Channel, and the weather.com website, Adnan felt he could get more personal with this couple.

"Double Click, may I ask why you have given such names to your children?"

"If we want to enter the twenty-first century, we can't do it with names like Faisal, or Henry."

"Why not?"

"These names are very old," said Double Click putting some salad into Adnan's plate. "Ancient. Why name our children after kings and queens? What have we in common with them? Royal families often killed each other and did terrible things. Tell me Adnan, would you like to name yourself after a serial killer?"

"No, never!"

"We know that Henry VIII killed his wives. We know that the Moghuls strangled their siblings to death. Yet we give our children their names."

"I must say that you make a good observation," said Adnan.

I nodded in agreement because the food was very good and I was more focused on the spicy chicken in my mouth than anything else.

Double Click explained his reasons. "We decided after moving to America that we would blend into the modern world and grab computer science as our way of life."

"Makes sense," said Hisaab Khan wanting to close the subject.

But Maaf Karna was still curious. "Forgive me, but don't the kids at school make fun of your children because of their names? Especially Mouse."

"Kids will be kids," said Monitor. "Mouse is doing so well in school."

"Yes," agreed Double Click. "His teachers love him. They say they can't do without him."

Monitor smiled happily at this and added, "He does all the computer work for the teachers. His best friend is a spread-sheet program. The teachers love Mouse!"

"So no one makes fun of him in school?"

"No, of course not," said Double Click. "Mouse is completely normal. He is scared of cats, though. But that is only natural for a boy his age."

Just then we heard the ring of a cell phone.

Double Click pulled out a small cell phone the size of a safety pin from his pocket and said, "Yes. Okay. Bye."

Just to break the ice a little bit, I joked, "Who was that? Your brother Right Click?"

"No, it was my nephew. He has a virus."

Everyone got serious and I felt embarrassed at attempting that kind of joke especially about a relative who was ill. Meanwhile Mouse and Keyboard were fighting, slapping each other's hands, and being disruptive. Double Click did not tolerate this insolence at the lunch table.

"I want both of you to go into sleep mode right now."

Both of the children lay on the floor and closed their eyes and became completely silent. We were impressed by this.

Adnan complimented him. "You control your children very well."

"Yes, we have a good operating system. Sometimes it crashes but overall it gets us through."

Adnan tried to break the ice into smaller pieces. "So Click, how did you meet your wife?"

"Oh, I want to tell the story! I want to tell," said Monitor. "What a scene it was!"

"We are so compatible," said Double Click, looking at his wife with all the affection that is possible at lunchtime. Monitor related the story with a thrill in her voice as she relived the moment.

"I was surrounded by these abusive, rowdy hooligans when he showed up," she said putting a loving hand on Double Click's shoulder.

Double Click smiled heroically. "I saw those guys were calling her names and being obnoxious. I told them to get lost."

Monitor got more romantic. "He fought them with these hands," she said holding his hands and gazing deep into his eyes as if looking into outer space at a twinkling star. Adnan was so impressed he put down the fork and clapped for Double Click. We joined in the applause, and the couple glowed with pride.

Adnan really admired Double Click for this. "What an adventure! I met my wife in a Chinese restaurant and it was all arranged. I had even reserved the table in advanced so nothing natural or spontaneous happened. They overcharged us for the fried rice but that was it. But you! You fought for your love! You rescued her from hooligans and thugs...that is really something. Well done, sir, well done."

"Oh yes, said Monitor, reliving the memory. "And the funny thing is that he had never clicked on me before."

"Forgive me, but I don't understand," said Maaf Karna.

"You know...messaged me." said Monitor in a soft romantic voice.

"Forgive me, but all this happened in a chat room?"

At this question both Monitor and Double Click laughed. Monitor looked at us as if we were crazy.

"Where else do things happen, silly?" She was very proud of Double Click. "His typing speed was so amazing, every one wanted him."

"Sixty words per minute," said Double Click. "Yep, these fingers have seen a lot of action."

"At that speed," said Monitor, mingling her fingers with his, "he could have had any girl in the chat room or any man pretending to be a girl. But these hands chose me."

The lunch ended with Adnan inviting them to the ARK. They had warmed up to us after telling us their story but remained reluctant to live on a large ship. Who could blame them?

"We can join you by video chat," they insisted. But Adnan remained firm and asked that they join us in reality.

Arrival

"Oh what a crazy Khan is he"

———————

DOUBLE CLICK Khan and several other leading families refused to join Adnan on the ARK. Adnan decided to reach out to the Desis by printing a front-page letter on *Hi There News*. It showed an image of the ARK and on one corner of the image, in a square, was Adnan's serious photograph in his captain's hat. Beneath this image were the words:

Dear Desis,
Come to the ARK and start a new life. The ARK is scheduled for launch on November 13.

Even then there was no response. Adnan spent the evenings dressed in his formal jacket and captain's hat, using a pair of heavy brass binoculars to scan the dock area for any visitors. But no one came.

At our breakfast meeting, Maaf Karna described the situation to Adnan. "Forgive me, but no one wants to live with you on a large ship."

Discouraging remarks were often followed by more negativity from Naureen. She now referred to Adnan as Crazy Khan. She even wrote some bad poetry and had the audacity to read it aloud when everyone was gathered for lunch.

I married a man, he is a Khan

Oh what a crazy Khan is he

Carries a chip

Big as a ship

Talks about his vision

Writes about his mission

In letters to Hercules

But try living with him

Then you will see

His real dream:

Avoiding all responsibility

———❦———

It was just like old times. Naureen was angry at Adnan. Adnan was chasing a dream. And the chance of everyone going to jail was always in the air. After such poetry sessions, Adnan often excused himself early from the dinner table and went for a walk, keeping his eyes on the docks.

Then it happened.

Recession came to America. The Desis had bought expensive homes thinking that they could sell them for even more. Some had bought more homes than they needed, as if they were buying coffee mugs. But as people defaulted on their mortgage payments the prices fell sharply. Banks took over the homes of people who could not pay their mortgage. This process, known as the foreclosure, was happening a lot. So often, in fact, that the word "foreclosure" became a common word of abuse. Instead of saying "oh snap" or "heck" people used the word "foreclosure" to express negative excitement. Sentences such as, "I don't give a foreclosure what you think," and "Where the foreclosure are my car keys?" were now heard.

The great housing crash led to loss of jobs, and many Desis became unemployed and desperate. We were standing on the deck of the ARK when we saw in the distance floating lights piercing the darkness like two angels in the night. As these got closer we realized it was a Japanese sedan. And behind it another. And behind it, several minivans. We saw a train of lights making their way from the highway all the way to the docks below us. There was yelling, honking, and shouting as the cars attempted to overtake each other, even though they were all coming to the same place. The Desis had arrived.

"You want to go beyond the normal"

———————

ON THE docks the Desi gathering was growing. Men, some casually dressed in sweat shirts and jeans, other men in suits; women, some in western clothing, others in saris and shalwar kameez; children with lollypops, elders with walking sticks, cooks in white aprons and puffy hats, painters with paintbrushes, musicians with guitars, and babies with rubber ducks. They were all here to board the ARK.

Adnan quickly made an assessment about the number of people on the docks. There was a spring in his step as he paced back and forth on the deck, thinking and talking in an inspired tone.

Maaf Karna tried to take control of the situation. "Forgive me, but we need to tell all those people to go back home. This ARK business is getting out of control. These people have taken your letters on *Hi There News* a little too seriously."

"I agree," said Hisaab Khan. "They are in the thousands. There is still a way out of this. Just tell them to leave right now."

How opposite were their thoughts from Adnan's.

"We are now leaders of a nation," said Adnan, who had obviously been preparing for this moment in his wild imagination. "The Desi League must lead by example. Everything we do now is part of history. When a thousand years have gone by and people look back, they will remember this moment."

"Forgive me, but how are we going to house all these people?" asked Maaf Karna.

"There are thousands of people out there and the number is growing," said Hisaab Khan. "Research has shown that people, when gathered in large groups, can become rowdy."

"Let's find out," said Adnan, adjusting his captain's hat for maximum neatness. He walked over to a control panel on the side of the control tower and flipped all the switches. As he did this, the massive ARK was filled with light. To the Desis gathered below it must have appeared as a glowing land in the sky. Adnan grabbed a loudspeaker and addressed them, his voice echoing on this historical night.

"I am Adnan Raheem Khan. Most of you know me from my letters."

"We know you from your mug shot when you were arrested," shouted a man from the docks.

"Yes, we have all struggled," continued Adnan. "You are all here for one reason," he said, his voice commanding their complete attention as they listened in silence. "You want to go beyond the normal. You want to explore and grow as human beings. You wish to be passengers on the ARK. But tell me this: Are we not all passengers?"

Most of the Desis did not really understand this question. They were here because they had defaulted on their mortgage or were avoiding phone calls from credit card companies and this was a free place to live.

"Here on this ARK," continued Adnan, "You are all welcome!"

The crowd was still silent.

"And," continued Adnan raising his voice to leader level, "there will be no rent!"

The crowd went wild. Loud cheers and clapping thundered from the docks. Even parrots that were with the Desis were clapping with their wings. All were relieved. Those sitting inside the cars honked melodiously to express satisfaction.

"Long live Adnan!" shouted one of them.

"You are all like my brothers and sisters," said Adnan, getting emotional.

There was more applause and a man shouted, "I think you are my cousin!"

"Yes, we are all like family," said Adnan. "Which is why it is important that we check your luggage for any dangerous materials. I also want you to know that you may not bring more than two suitcases each. And each suitcase must not exceed thirty pounds."

At this the crowd responded with shouts of defiance. "How can that be? We are Desis. We are Desis!"

The women in the crowd were most angered by this. They created a weight problem. Not because they were fat but because of their luggage.

"We shall not comply with your request," shouted a woman who was sitting comfortably on her luggage. All around her were more suitcases bursting with fullness. "Each woman here has fifteen suitcases."

Adnan tried to reason. "Oh, Desi women, why do you bring to the ARK, your new home, so many suitcases? Do you not know the limit is two suitcases each? Why do you exceed the weight allotted to you?"

The same woman now spoke as the representative of all the women present. Her voice was loud and defiant. "Each of us shall bring fifteen suitcases apiece, and each suitcase shall be most heavy."

"Why?" asked Adnan. He was facing his first crisis as a leader of the Desis.

195

"Because in these suitcases we carry the dresses we wore on our weddings. And also the dresses we wore at other weddings and the dresses that we might wear in future weddings."

"But what need do you have for them on the ARK?"

There was a pause and everyone waited for the woman to respond. She did so in the most convincing manner. "We have no daily use of these things. But on weekends we like to unpack these suitcases and unfold these dresses, stare at them and then fold them back again. It is what we do."

"But did you not leave Pakistan twenty-five years ago? Surely the fashion has changed."

"Indeed it has," said the woman. "But we haven't."

At this witty reply all the Desis clapped loudly. Seeing that this was the will of the people, Adnan gave in.

"You may bring all your suitcases," he said.

The crowd considered this a great victory and congratulated each other. As a leader, Adnan had won them over. In other boring places like airports and train stations, Desi women were unable to express their true nature and adapted to limitations. But here on the ARK Adnan recognized their human rights and allowed them to bring all fifteen suitcases which contained important parts of their personality.

But soon this cheerful rejoicing among the men turned into deep anguish, because great was the burden on them. As husbands, brothers, and sons, it was they who had to carry these heavy suitcases to the ARK. At first they were upbeat about it, even cracking jokes and saying to the women, "Oh, fifteen suitcases are nothing." But their happiness faded quickly into sadness as they picked up the luggage. As they struggled forward with these heavy things they asked, "What is inside these?" Some grew so tired they crawled forward on their hands and knees as the suitcases weighed them down. Some of the men cried loudly because they wanted to be macho and carry two suitcases at one time. And while they carried these suitcases, women placed heavy leather bags around their necks like necklaces of pain. Their mothers, wives, and sisters urged them onward as the men, burdened by all this luggage, walked like penguins. Many were the tears and shades of red on their exhausted faces.

As there was no space in the cabins for these thousands of suitcases, the men piled the suitcases on the deck one upon the other. When thousands of suitcases had been piled up, they took the shape of a large step pyramid similar in appearance to the early pyramids seen in ancient Egypt.

Adnan, who had seen something similar in the history section of the bookstore, saw this as a good sign. He climbed this huge pyramid of suitcases until he reached the top. Standing on a sturdy orange suitcase he yelled in joy. "Oh, Desis of the ARK, our culture is taking shape. We are creating our own architecture!" The women responded with clapping but the men were too tired to respond and lay on the deck catching their breath.

The Desi cooks were the most welcome. They walked with pride, for they knew they had the skill to produce joy and chicken tikka.

"Welcome," said Adnan as the cooks walked in. All Desis pulled out rugs forming a long carpet upon which the cooks entered the ARK. "Truly," said Adnan looking at a cook, "you are loved."

Like true professionals the cooks went to work, quickly placing bricks on top of each other creating two towers. The space between these towers they filled with coal. Their assistants marinated chicken in spicy yogurt while another lit the coal with a matchstick. To keep the coals burning he waved a Japanese-style fan. It was mesmerizing to see the coals changing colors, sometimes red, sometimes not. The chicken was soon on the grill, the juices falling off into the coals creating sizzle and smoke. The charcoal smoke filled the ARK with a familiar fragrance that spoke to the soul of every Desi. They were home.

Among the crowd were children. Happy boys with shaved heads dressed in oversized shirts and safari suits. Desis anticipate the future by buying oversized clothes for their children so that the children can grow into them all their lives. Small shy girls in oversized ball gowns and heavy eye makeup made their way onto the deck and sat on blankets, leaning against their large, serious-looking mothers. Elders with prayer beads came and took their place on the blankets resting their elbows on cylindrical pillows. The smoke from the chicken tikka spread on the ARK in clouds of delight.

The first to arrive on the ARK were those who had lost their homes to foreclosures. The news of the ARK spread so fast that even those families that had once snubbed Adnan's invitations now came over out of curiosity and for the food, which was becoming legend.

Some of the more prominent Desis included the Muftas. They were a well-known couple who had made a living in America by not spending any money. Mr. Mufta explained his lifestyle. "Do you know we have never paid for lunch or dinner?"

"How do you achieve this?" asked an admirer.

"We go to the best organic grocery stores."

"But those are expensive!"

"We only eat the highest-quality foods. We go there and we keep sampling until our stomachs are full." The small crowd that had gathered around them clapped at this, and some guests even expressed the desire to do the same.

"What other things do you not pay for?"

"Clothes. We go to local universities and fill out credit card applications. For this we receive choices of free items such as T-shirts, coffee mugs. At my house I only keep the newest electronic equipment. After thirty days I return it and get something else."

We all thanked Mr. Mufta for sharing his knowledge with us. He was a healthy-looking man, and he wore a dark brown jacket valued at $79.65. We knew this because he had not taken the tag off.

Literal Desi arrived on the ARK without any apologies for his past behavior. He had been released from prison and now wished to be a resident of the ARK. Double Click Khan arrived with his wife Monitor, and their kids, Mouse and Keyboard.

Adnan personally welcomed this modern family. "Welcome Double Click! Welcome Monitor!"

Double Click Khan smiled nervously. "We are here to scan reality. It's really challenging to meet all these people. On video chat it is much easier." But he seemed happy. Mouse and Keyboard had already met Bubloo and Tina, and they were taking turns jumping from the pyramid.

"Then what can you say in defense of this wild and cruel man?"

T HE LARGE ARK had many cabins. Since most of these were under the deck, Adnan allowed the Desis to settle in wherever they liked. We heard some shouting and fighting but we decided to ignore those unpleasant things as they were happening below the deck. Life on the ARK took on its own shape. Here I will mention two incidents that happened.

One evening Adnan climbed up the pyramid to speak into a microphone that had been installed on the highest suitcase.

"We have all settled in to the ARK. I know you have complaints about some people taking more space or others having a better view from their cabins. But these are small things…"

He was interrupted by a man holding his hand up. "May I have the microphone please?"

"Just after I finish," said Adnan.

But the man simply smiled and grabbed the microphone from Adnan's hands. He now addressed the Desis. "I have a very talented nephew and he would like to perform on stage. He is only fourteen years old but the level of musical maturity he has displayed has left us astounded. I would like a drummer and a guitarist to please come onto the pyramid."

Two men, one with a guitar and the other with a drum set took their places on the pyramid stage.

"And now, ladies and gentlemen, please welcome Kamran Khan!"

A boy dressed in black jeans and a yellow shirt climbed on the stage. He wore large white joggers that covered his ankles and his tight jeans disappeared into them. A calculator digital watch, which was waterproof up to 300 hundred meters in case something bad happened, was visible on his hand.

He took the microphone and bowed to the audience. "Today I would like to perform ABC."

"What?" protested an audience member. "He is fourteen years old. ABC is for babies. Is he okay?"

"Shut up," shouted the uncle. "Have some feelings. Yes, he is an artist. He received high marks in all his classes and his handwriting is neat. So just give him a chance."

Like a professional, the boy nodded at the supporting musicians. He then spoke to the guitarist. "I will sing ABC, and you will provide support by guitar. Your fingers will play the strings like an ancient Egyptian palace servant hired to massage the hair of the Pharaoh Queen Cleopatra."

Then the boy turned to the drummer. "I will sing ABC, and I want you to hit the drums like you are witnessing the birth of a star safely from another galaxy while eating gelato."

The drummer hit his drums with great enthusiasm making the *dha dhaa dhish* sound.

And then in his pure voice the fourteen-year-old Kamran Khan unleashed a song that conquered our doubts and made us worshippers of melody. *"Aay Beee Seee Deee Eeee Aaf Geeeee..."*

The boy had already reached a pitch that award-winning singers could only reach if they had the support of a national space agency and they allowed the singers to use their space shuttle with extra boosters. The drummer hit the drums like there was no tomorrow or yesterday, and all our hearts were beating with it. The guitarist, also inspired by this song, strummed the strings with all his passion.

The fourteen-year-old continued in a voice that nature gifted to mankind. *"Aich I Jay Kay Aaalo Mano Peeeee..."*

The sound of 'Peee' lifted the delighted audience like a helicopter. Our spirits became angels who used the clouds as high-quality mattresses.

Then Kamran Khan went into reverse gear to gather momentum. *"Alo Mano Peee kyoo Our Ass Teeeeee..."*

Some in the audience were crying.

Then, using his shoes to perform a sliding reverse walk, he delivered the last line with more passion than Samson had for Delilah. *"You We Double You Ax Why Zed?"*

We rose to our feet clapping and shouting our admiration. He had given to the Western alphabet an Eastern soul. He had achieved in one song what leaders and thinkers had attempted for thousands of years.

Adnan climbed the pyramid and patted this boy on the shoulder. He waited for the applause to die down. "Well done, son! Well done! You have made everyone here very proud." He handed the boy a key chain which had a small flashlight attached to it. "This is my gift to you. The light will always be with you, as long as you keep changing the battery."

But life on the ARK wasn't all fun, games, and doughnuts. Some bad things did happen. I don't wish to chocolate coat and sprinkle diced almonds on everything. The truth must be told. One of the residents was Janglee Janwar or JJ as he was known. The trouble began on *Movie Night Tuesday* when we had gathered to see a love story filmed in Paris. JJ showed up wearing a sombrero and sat in the front row. He blocked everyone's view. People sitting on the left could only see the hero, people sitting on the right could only see the heroine, and no one could see the beauty of Paris. When we asked JJ to take off the sombrero, he exclaimed, "It's my culture," even though he had nothing to do with Mexico.

For a while complaints had been coming in to Adnan about this man. Adnan ignored the problem, hoping that it would go away. But JJ continued his antics. Whenever Desis hung their clothes to dry on the clothesline, JJ would steal these clothes and make mops out of them, which he used to sweep and clean his area of the deck. "Nice shirt," he would compliment someone and then follow it by saying, "It's going to make a good mop." At meal times he liked to throw the naan like a frisbee across the long tables, disturbing every-one. In those early days the residents lived in tents on the deck of the ARK. At night JJ would sneak into these tents, slap people who were sleeping, and then run away laughing loudly, saying, "It wasn't me, you were having a nightmare." When confronted in the morning by angry Desis who had been slapped, JJ would shrug his shoulders and shout, "I was just playing with you! It's just a hobby, nothing serious." He was a real pain for everyone in the literal sense because he also kicked people and when cornered always claimed that he was "just kidding."

One day JJ pushed some people overboard because he was bored. We heard a loud splash, followed by a victorious shout by JJ, "Just kidding! I'm just playing." Later on at a motivational talk where the speaker encouraged everyone to "just believe in yourself and go for it," JJ took things to a new level. He doused parts of the ship in kerosene and set it on fire. Luckily the fire was stopped just in time, though considerable parts of the Viking floor were damaged. Finally Adnan took action. He ordered the Desis to surround JJ and bring him to justice. It was Literal Desi who actually caught JJ. This is an official record of JJ's trial.

The man appointed judge in this case had once worked at a dial-up Internet provider company. At the height of his career when Internet was accessed through the telephone, he was happily employed and admired. But with the rise of high-speed Internet, he had been left behind. He had come to the ARK in a dejected state, unshaven, hair uncombed, hoping for a second chance at life. We had welcomed him and made him a Desi by first feeding him nihari and then teaching him to ask deeply personal questions at parties, questions such as "So when are you finally getting married?" He had a good deep voice and he served in the ARK as the official announcer for lunch, dinner, and important events. Because of his good voice, Adnan promoted him to judge. Today he sat on a high chair as the citizens of the ARK made their case against JJ.

"Your Honor, this man has been like a wolf among sheep. He slaps us while we sleep. He has kicked many of us. He steals our clothes and mops the dirty deck with them. He tried to burn the ship. We demand that this man be expelled from the ARK."

JJ, who had indeed done such things, happened to have a very good lawyer. The lawyer, who had once worked as a manager at a photocopying store, knew how to make excuses for jobs done badly. He addressed the legal gathering in his roundabout manner.

"Your Honor, I admit that JJ has some quirks. He likes to slap people while they sleep. And yes, Your Honor, my client is not perfect. He tried to burn down the ship. I also admit that he pulled your hair as soon as he entered the courtroom. That was wrong. I mean, it must have been painful."

"Just get to the point," said the judge.

"Your Honor, our defense is solid."

"How can that be? You just admitted to a number of crimes. Never in my career has anyone pulled my hair, even when I worked for a dial-up Internet company."

"Your Honor, when you and the jury hear this defense they will be convinced that my client is innocent."

"Are you pleading insanity?"

"No, Your Honor."

"Then what can you say in defense of this wild and cruel man?"

"Your Honor," he said looking toward the angry residents of the ARK, "No matter what he does, *Yeh dil ke bahut achay hain.* (He has a good heart). There was a stunned silence. The people who had been complaining against JJ now softened. On their faces an understanding expression took over. In Desi culture, a man may make a few mistakes such as burning down a neighborhood or shooting people in anger. But if he has a good heart, then people are willing to accept him. The crowds who had been shouting for the banishment of JJ were now calling for his release.

"Let him go. Let him go, you villains. He has a good heart. Let him go." Even before the judge could give his judgment, the crowd carried JJ on their shoulders, shouting slogans that celebrated his personality.

In those early days, the residents gathered together to thank God that they had a home on the ARK at a time of recession. But an argument arose when the method of thanking God was challenged by those who claimed to know the technical details on the procedure for thanking. "There is only one way to do it, and it is our way."

They were of course challenged by others who claimed to have a perfect user manual on the thanking procedures. These debates became so severe that opposing groups met at different times to be grateful. When one group was thanking God, the other group was dancing, which offended the worshipers. Some creative folks attempted to combine gratitude with dancing, but this innovation was angrily rejected by all groups as too happy.

Then there were the atheists. Although they had walked out of religion, they still participated in the festivals. "We still like the food," they would say. They too were hated by believers in both factions. These differences were growing, and sometimes we woke up in the mornings to find offensive slogans spray-painted on the deck—confusing slogans such as *"Fight for peace."* The fighting became so frequent that on some nights we avoided going out of the control tower. One night Adnan invited Double Click Khan to dinner to discuss the worsening situation. Double Click described the Desi situation on the ARK in his own special manner.

"Mr. Adnan, putting Desis together in one place is like buying a three-in-one printer that claims to be a scanner as well as a copier. It always breaks down."

"Is it time for an FBI raid?"

A DNAN COUNTERED the situation with a speech and a plan.

"I will make you a great nation," he said in a speech to all residents of the ARK before a dinner party. Everyone clapped loudly in hopes that applause would end the speech and dinner would be served. But Adnan made a historical announcement. "And so on this day I announce the *Work or Leave Program*."

The residents of the ARK were deeply divided against each other, but no one wanted to go back to paying rent. They took the *Work or Leave Program* very seriously, epecially Literal Desi, who was promoted to manager. Janglee Janwar became an enforcer. The residents accepted Janglee Janwar as an authority because they knew that deep down, he had a good heart.

Under this program the Desis would transform the ARK into a modern living space. The details of brainstorming, building, painting, hammering, welding, scraping, twisting, stretching, slapping, and spontaneous dancing are too many to recount here. All I am going to say is that in just one year, the Desis of the ARK had achieved a miracle. And during all this time Adnan had forbidden all residents to leave this great ship. All supplies in and out of the ARK were handled personally by the Desi League high command, which included only Adnan, Maaf Karna, Hisaab Khan, and me. This privilege made me very popular, and many residents of the ARK requested favors from me, asking me to get them this lamp for their cabin or that favorite breakfast cereal.

The press had become very curious about the ARK, but our policy was to say nothing to the journalists. The media hated to be left out of anything and printed sensational headlines.

> *What are they doing on that ship?*
> *Is he building a weapon?*
> *Is it time for an FBI raid?*
> *Why does he do such things?*

One day, Adnan put an end to all the speculation when he invited one reporter for an official tour of the ARK. This reporter once had her own talk show. And though retired from television, she still had the curiosity for a good story and accepted Adnan's invitation.

With this famous reporter arriving to tour the Ark, a lot of excitement was created in the media. Hundreds of journalists and cameramen camped on the docks facing the ARK, eating their energy bars and drinking their strong coffees. But Adnan had found a way to bypass all of them. The reporter arrived by helicopter.

Official Tour

"It is a state of joy"

———◆———

THE REPORTER spoke to the world from the helicopter as it hovered above the ARK. No cameras were allowed to accompany her and the whole world relied on her voice to learn the secrets of the ARK.

"Ladies and gentlemen, I am in a helicopter that will be landing on the mysterious ARK, home to fifteen thousand people. We are now flying over the ARK. Oh my God, I don't believe it. I see a very large garden in the middle. This is a floating island, folks. Our helicopter is now landing on what appears to be an oval garden in which several men wearing white are standing around aimlessly."

"They call this cricket," said the helicopter pilot.

"Cricket! They have a cricket ground on the ship. How strange!"

Was it strange? If ships can have billiard tables, chandeliers, and a disco, then what was so strange about a cricket ground? The helicopter landed in the middle of the oval-shaped lawn covered with lime-green grass that had been cut to perfection. If there was one thing that the Desis loved without hesitation it was cricket. They considered this holy ground and lovingly took care of every blade of grass.

As the reporter got out of the helicopter she noticed that all the seats around the stadium were empty. "Where are the people?"

The sound of trumpets broke the silence in a royal manner. A booming voice on a loudspeaker announced: "Adnan Raheem Khan, Defender of Joy, Conqueror of Highway 635, Solver of Problems, Dreamer of Dreams, is now arriving!"

Adnan entered the cricket ground on a chariot pulled by two magnificent brown horses that had grown up in Kentucky and were now celebrated members of the ARK animal community. Adnan was standing on the chariot while the driver—with a shaved head and a maroon gown made from a bed sheet with a high thread count—held the reins of the horses. Adnan was dressed in his navy-blue blazer, khaki pants, and a crisp white shirt. On his head was the captain's hat, which symbolized his complete authority over the ARK and its residents. He also wore a small hidden microphone so his every word would echo all over the ARK and even reach the pier where the press was camped. The magnificent horses galloped toward the reporter as she stood there in anticipation. The chariot stopped smartly in front of her.

Adnan got out and announced "The Desis of the ARK welcome you."

At this command, thousands of Desis appeared in the stands. Where there was silence only moments ago, now there was a roaring applause. Every where she looked, the reporter saw people, some holding signs of welcome and others waving flags.

"Where did they come from?"

"They were hiding under their seats to surprise you," explained Adnan.

"I am shocked!" she replied. "I have never experienced anything like this. How did you get so many of these people to join you on the ARK?"

"I suppose I have inspired them by calling them to a higher purpose."

Adnan was right. These people had flocked to the ARK because they needed his leadership and were desperate to avoid the credit card and mortgage payments.

"All this is very formal!" said the reporter.

"This is an official State visit," said Adnan with a smile.

"But this ARK is not a state. It is a ship."

"It is a state of joy," said Adnan.

We had been instructed to clap at anything witty he said. We all clapped, adding intensity to the conversation between the guest and her host. The reporter took her place on the chariot and stood next to Adnan. The people cheered as the horses galloped around the stadium, giving the people in the stands a closer look at the famous reporter. They galloped out of the stadium, and now the secrets of the ARK would be revealed to an outsider for the first time.

"In their hearts they wish robots would do it"

⊱━━━⊰

THE FIRST stop on the ARK was a large silver-colored building about four stories high. The structure was shiny and metallic. In the middle of this building was a large round window that covered most of the building.

"What is this strange-looking building?" asked the reporter.

"This is where we do laundry," said Adnan with a hint of pride.

"This whole building is a washing machine?"

"Yes we decided that in order to create a decent society we should wash all our clothes in the same machine. And so our scientific team created the world's largest washing machine. Fifty thousand clothing items can be washed in one load."

"Are such things possible?"

"You are just in time to witness how it is done. In our day-to-day lives, we say a prayer of thanks before we eat food, but when it comes to washing our clothes we lose our gratitude. Humanity approaches laundry as a boring task. Their faces become neutral and in their hearts they wish robots would do it. Here on the ARK we are more grateful."

A middle-aged bald man, who had been chosen for having the shiniest head on the ARK, came forward. As the laundry high priest he wore a white robe to symbolize purity and the power of bleach.

"May the detergent wash away all your stains!" he said loudly.

Three men and three women, carefully selected for their strength, came running forward and attached ropes to hooks on this great machine. Using these ropes they pulled open the great round glass door. A well-built man, the only one on the ARK who had regularly lifted weights, was now beating a large drum. *Boom Boom Boom Boom.* To this rhythm the door with the gigantic glass window opened slowly. Everyone stood at attention with their right hand on their heart. A long line of Desis had already formed. Thousands stood with bags of laundry in their hands.

"Loading will now begin," said the laundry high priest. "Let the waters run through the fabric, let the detergent scrub them clean."

The Desis came forward one by one, balancing their bags of laundry on their heads. One nervous boy who was distracted by the reporter turned his head to look at her. The bag of clothes slipped from his head and dropped to the ground. He quickly picked up the bag and ran away with it.

The reporter was puzzled by the boy's behavior. "What happened? Where did he go?"

"To the back of the line," said the laundry high priest with authority.

"But why?"

"Our laws state that clothes to be washed must be carried on the head. Only then will they be accepted in the washing machine."

"But why?"

"This prevents us from overloading the machine. There is only that much they can carry on their head," said the priest with pride.

Upon reaching the great round glass door, the Desis tilted their heads dropping their bags of laundry respectfully into the hands of the loading priests. The loading priests were dressed in different colored robes representing the universal and colorful nature of laundry.

The loading priests took bags one by one from the residents, looked inside each bag, and passed personal remarks. "Looks like you dropped coffee all over your shirt. And when you eat chocolate cake do you also like to feed it to the sweat shirt? That white shirt—if you can call it that—has sweat stains so large its looks like a disgusting map of the world. And look at those socks. Did you go mud skating?"

The residents became embarrassed, and shame filled their faces. And just when they were ready to cry, the loading priest would say, "But fear not, all your clothes are accepted."

At this, the relieved and happy resident would reply, "Thank you! I am unburdened."

After this exchange, the loading priests emptied these bags of dirty laundry into the machine. This continued until the machine was filled with thousands of clothes. The door was closed ceremoniously by the door team to the beating of drums.

The laundry high priest walked over to the reporter. "We, the people of the ARK, ask you to pour the detergent and select the wash cycle."

"This is the highest honor that could be given to a non-Desi," said Adnan. He gestured toward an elevator leading to the top of this gigantic machine.

The reporter, accompanied by Adnan and the laundry high priest, stepped onto the elevator. As they ascended they were watched silently by the residents. Here on the top of this massive machine was a wheelbarrow full of translucent blue gleaming detergent. It gave off the fragrance of snow-covered mountains. The reporter pushed the wheelbarrow toward a square opening on the roof of the machine. She tilted the wheelbarrow and the thick liquid fell into the opening like a small waterfall. Next, the reporter used both of her hands to turn the giant knob to *medium-cold wash, colors.*

"And now we must go down," said the laundry high priest.

"But I still have not started the machine," said the reporter, who was now really getting into it. She was pointing to the red start button on the control panel.

"I am afraid only the laundry high priest has that privilege," said Adnan.

And so they came down, leaving the high priest standing on top of the machine. As everyone stood at attention, the laundry high priest pushed the large red button and experienced an immense sense of power. The washing had begun.

Through the large glass door it was all visible. Thousands of clothes tumbled in a circular motion. Water filled the massive machine, submerging the clothes, mixing with the detergent to create white, soapy foam that clung like snow to the inner surface of the massive glass door.

The reporter made a confession. "I never felt that doing laundry could be so meaningful. This truly is amazing! There are tons of clothes being washed at the same time!"

"Yes," said Adnan. "This is why we call this machine the *Washington.* From it we derive our inalienable right to be free from the tyranny of dry cleaners."

Farming & Science

"You have made history"

———◆———

AFTER *WASHINGTON*, Adnan accompanied the reporter to a tall glass building we had constructed. "These must be your offices," guessed the reporter. "Here you probably do all the paper work, such as accounting and administrative tasks. It must be full of telephones and fax machines, computers and coffee machines."

"Why don't you enter and find out?" said Adnan.

As we entered the building the reporter shouted. "I smell strawberries!"

"Because you are standing in our farm," said Adnan. "We grow our food inside this building."

"Inside a building?"

"Yes, it is a silly thing that in this modern age crops should depend on seasons. Indoor farming allows us to grow crops throughout the year."

We took the elevator, which stopped on different floors named:

Vegetables & Fruits

Nuts

Rice & Wheat

We got off on the *Vegetables & Fruits* floor, which was the most impressive. It was easy to pluck edible things from the trees around us. The reporter picked a strawberry and found it to be very tasty.

"This indoor farm provides employment to the residents of the ARK," said Adnan. "And yet our farmers are not isolated on large fields but work right here in this building. In doing this we have made farming an urbane, modern, and community-based exercise. As you know, very few soap operas celebrate the life of farmers because they are not considered glamorous. In large fields, where workers barely bump into each other, there is very little interaction. But here inside this indoor farm, because of their constant interaction, the workers gossip about one another and feel more engaged." He pointed to a group of farmers in denim overalls talking at a water cooler. "See them? They are probably talking about you right now, even though they are smiling politely."

"City farming is a very modern concept," agreed the reporter. She noticed that some people were walking around the plants with musical instruments while others were reading from a paper. "Who are they?"

"They are reaping the benefits of this farm. In the Desi community, students have three options. They may study medicine, they may become engineers, or they may commit suicide. Art and music are subjects often neglected by the Desis. Artists are not considered productive members of society. Their parents ask them, "If you study music or creative arts, how will you feed yourself?""

"That is so sad!" said the reporter.

"It is indeed, and what a tragedy. But no more! Science has shown that plants grow faster and healthier when in the presence of music and caring conversation. So there sits a musician playing guitar to the broccoli. There you see a girl playing the saxophone to a group of carrots. And over there a writer is reading his fiction to a bunch of tomatoes. Look at their faces! How happy they are!"

"Yes they do seem happy."

"And now look at the faces of the writers and singers! How proud they look! While being artistic they are helping the food grow. Here in this farm, we have made the artists productive members of society. Their music is nourishing us. Also no longer must the artists starve because they may eat any member of their audience."

"These are very new ideas! I must say your ARK offers unique solutions to the problems of this world."

"I try," said Adnan. He was attempting modesty but it was difficult for him. "There is one more thing I would like you to see."

"What is that?" asked the reporter. Her eyes twinkled with anticipation.

"I would like to take you to the science labs. There we develop the most cutting-edge technologies."

"Forgive me," interrupted Maaf Karna, "but I thought no one was allowed to go in that building?"

"I think now the time has come," said Adnan. This was exciting, because for one year—during the great construction—only Adnan and a few scientists had gone into that building. Not even the Desi League high council had been allowed.

We exited the vertical farm and followed them to the small single-story building. This was the *Institute of Research and Development.* As soon as we entered the building we were confronted by an elevator.

"Forgive me, but why do we have an elevator inside a one storied building?"

Adnan ignored Maaf Karna and pushed the number seven button. The elevator was descending. This was a top secret building, much deeper than we had assumed. The elevator door opened to reveal a large room bustling with hectic activity. Men and women in white lab coats carrying test tubes and conical flasks walked briskly from here to there. Some carried large calculators and some made jokes that only they understood.

The chief scientist among them saw us and approached Adnan excitedly. "Sir, I believe the machine is complete exactly to your specifications."

Adnan held the chief scientist by the shoulders. "If this is correct, we have made history."

"What is it?" asked the reporter in excitement. "What have you made?"

"Follow me," said the scientist.

We followed him through a long corridor and passed through several swinging doors, finally reaching the maximum security area. The steel door looked like an entrance to a vault. The scientist placed his chin on a biometric device embedded on the wall.

An electronic voice responded, *Your double chin has been recognized. You may enter.*

The door slid open. In the middle of this secure room was an object the size of a small car covered with a black cloth.

"What is that?" asked the reporter.

"It will all be clear very soon," said the scientist. He took a small radio from his lab coat pocket. "Please send me the Desi subject. We are ready to experiment." In just a few moments a healthy-looking man in his late thirties with a serious face joined us in this lab.

The reporter wanted to know who this man was.

"This man," said the scientist, "has been selected because he has all the traits of an average Desi. He will be testing our machine."

The man looked both nervous and eager.

"As you know," said Adnan, "we Desis like to feel sorry for ourselves. We are most lucky—our stomachs are full and we have shelter and safety and toothpaste so that there is no friction when the toothbrush slides over our teeth. We have these things and yet we complain."

"Forgive me," interrupted Maaf Karna, "but ingratitude is our defining feature."

"Yes," agreed Hisaab Khan, "I complain at least fifteen times a day."

"Yes, it is true," said Adnan. "But don't you think it becomes a little difficult to complain when we come to America?"

The reporter watched our conversation with great attention.

The Desi subject who had been brought in to test the machine now spoke. "In America, you have to work hard. Get up early...the weather keeps changing. Every one is too busy and they don't have time for you. You have to call people before you visit them. I hate that! Where is the surprise?"

"Yes," said Adnan.

"Go on, you are on the right track," said the scientist to the Desi subject in an encouraging manner.

"Everyone gets into this immigrant energy," he said. "Some Desis no longer have the time to visit you and feel for you. When I do meet them and tell them my problems they say, 'okay, here's the solution,' or 'go to that therapist,' or talk to that counselor, or read this self-help book, or join that seminar. I mean, where is the sympathy?"

"Exactly! They have lost the way," said the scientist. He walked toward the object in the middle of the room. Pulling the cloth away, he revealed the machine. It looked like a driving arcade game in which people can sit and play. The scientist announced with pride, "I present you the Afsose (sympathy) Machine, Model 9000."

The scientist took the Desi man's blood pressure. Then it was time. The Desi subject sat in the machine. Seat belts automatically came out and strapped him in firmly.

The machine addressed the Desi subject in a soothing female robotic voice.

Welcome to Afsose Machine 9000. Please enter twenty-five million dollars to start the machine.

"But I don't have twenty-five million dollars." he said in a sad voice.

What did you say?

"I said I don't have twenty-five million dollars."

Awww, you poor thing.

The machine had started expressing sympathy. It was interactive.

You poor thing! You must be feeling so tired!

Then came the sounds of a child crying. *Ooowaaahhh Ooowwaaahhh.* This was accompanied by the sound of a woman sniffling followed by the sound of a man saying, *Your luck is bad, your luck is bad. Everyone is against you. Everyone is planning against you. What's the point of trying, anyway?*

Then mechanical rubber hands emerged from the side of the machine and patted the man on the head. All this while the sounds of the baby crying continued. Then a hiccup, then sentences like, *So many bad things happened to you, only you. Ooooowaaaaah. Hiccup. Hands. Awwww.*

The Desi subject was crying. Tears were falling from his eyes. This continued for approximately five minutes. He cried with all his heart and allowed the Afsose machine to completely take over his brain. And then it was over. Everything stopped and the machine made this announcement.

Self-pity is now complete. Thank you for using Afsose Machine 9000.

We rushed to the machine and surrounded the man. He opened the seatbelt and got out from the machine. The scientist held him by the shoulders.

"Well how was it?" Did it work?"

"Did it work, you ask," said the man enthusiastically. "This machine is amazing! I feel great! Ever since I moved to America I wanted to do this but no one had the time! This is so good. Now I don't have to wait for people to feel sorry for me. I just strap myself into this and the Afsose machine takes care of all the sympathy I am seeking. When can I come back?"

There was celebration in the room. The scientist shook hands with all of us and Adnan said, "We have created history!"

"It's a winner," I said to the scientist. "Let's send this to every Desi in America. I know there is a huge market in the subcontinent and in the Middle East as well. They will love it over there."

"No they won't," said the scientist.

"Why not? It's so convenient, and it's automatic!"

"No," he said. "They prefer manual."

"Perhaps like our great leader Adnan he was feeling the burden of history"

—————◆—————

IWAS ON the deck of the ARK on a Sunday morning playing hide and seek with some girls who, after reaching the age of thirty-five, were now allowed to play with boys. I noticed a black SUV with federal government license plate parked on the dock. A man in a black suit and dark glasses waved at us.

"I come from the White House," he shouted.

"Which one?" I asked. "There are so many. White is a very popular color and sits well on wood as well as cement. It is the color of choice for those who are indecisive."

"Thee White House," he replied in old English.

Hearing this, Maaf Karna got up. "Forgive me for saying this, but why have you come to the ARK?"

"To deliver this," said the man in the black suit. He took out a bottle from his jacket and threw it at us. The bottle sailed toward us in a perfect arc and I caught it easily as if it were hanging by a thread in the air. The man drove away. Everyone gathered around me to look at the bottle closely. It was an elegant green glass bottle. I pulled the cork and took out a yellow scroll of paper. It held words in deep-blue ink. Someone with good handwriting had written it.

To the Desi League,
As you know that our country is facing a financial crisis.
In building the ARK you have gathered thousands of people
to your cause. It is rumored that you plan to leave with them.
I invite you to join me for a meeting to discuss these serious
matters.
Sincerely,
The President of the United States

When we read the letter to Adnan, he was thrilled. "Yes! Finally we are being recognized at the highest levels of government. There was a time, gentlemen, when the mailman brought bills and some coupons and always that heavy phone book with unneeded numbers. But today we have received an invitation from the White House." Adnan was eager to respond quickly but at the same time he wanted his reply to have everything: sophistication, punctuation, and perfect spelling.

Maaf Karna got too involved with this process. "Forgive me for saying this, but I think it's important to consider the language very carefully."

"Yes," said Hisaab Khan. "We must read the final draft at least ten times before sending it."

"I am very happy to be invited to the White House," said Adnan. "I want to express that."

"Make a smiley face with a nice thick black marker," I said.

"That will set the mood," said Adnan considering my suggestion as he drew a big smiley face on the paper.

But Maaf Karna and Hisaab Khan overruled my suggestion.

"Forgive me, but we are not teenagers, though Minhaj is mentally fourteen. If we send a smiley face to the White House, they will not take us seriously."

"Or worse," added Hisaab Khan, "it could trigger an equal but opposite reaction from the White House. Their response might include a face with an inverse smile."

Only Hisaab Khan could take the fun out of a smiley face. And Maaf Karna was his usual self, an assassin of joy who never misses. He falls among those people who try to act cool under all circumstances. Like people at the airport when they are using the moving walkway and even though it is moving for them and they are having fun, on their faces we still see a frown. I hate people who try to act cool by hiding their happiness.

Adnan wanted to accommodate all our views in his response. The final draft came to be:

Dear Mr. President,
We accept your invitation with cautious delight.

The letter went to the White House and a few days later we received security clearance to see the President.

Our excitement level remained very high as we flew to Washington, DC. Everyone drank a lot of orange juice and Adnan made notes, staring at times deeply into the clouds from his window seat. When we reached the White House after lunch we were taken straight to the Oval Office.

When we entered the Oval Office, the President did not see us. He was facing the window behind his desk. The light enveloped his dark-blue suit and his face was illuminated like copper. It seemed to me that he was lost in deep thoughts. Perhaps like our great leader, Adnan, he was feeling the burden of history. He soon realized he was not alone and turned around to face us. Though his face still held other thoughts he smiled to wipe them away.

"Welcome! And thank you for coming here to see me," he said in his firm, commanding voice.

We shook hands with him. Adnan sat on a chair while Maaf Karna, Hisaab Khan, and I sat on the beige-colored sofa. The president took a seat on a leather chair placing one leg over the other in his lean elegant manner. We were hanging out with the most powerful man on earth. I could also smell something tasty.

"I ordered some special cupcakes for you," said the president. "Please have some." he nodded toward a tray of cupcakes on the table in front of us. This was a wise move. Cupcakes are tools of diplomacy. In Washington, DC, people in tight clothes and new hairstyles stand in a long line outside fashionable cupcake stores to simply get in.

Counting the president we were five people, so mathematics and universal morality dictated that each of us should have eaten two cupcakes. But when I ate the chocolate-covered cupcake, I realized that I did not have the character, the capacity for sacrifice, or the willpower to stick to my two-cupcake limit. Besides, the president never said, "Oh, here are ten cupcakes, we are five, so we get two each." He was too nice. It was a sophisticated gathering and we all considered ourselves above the counting of food. I ate six.

The conversation turned to the ARK. The president expressed his concern directly. "I think you have to consider all the good things about America before you make plans to leave it for some unknown land."

"It is a voyage of discovery, Mr. President. We need to find our own way."

"America is a big country and there are many things here that you can discover. They are serving palak paneer at the grocery store! What more would you like?"

"We want less. We want to strip away all the luxuries, and the roads, and the comforts. We wish to discover nature in lush green surroundings filled with streams and waterfalls."

"That is a good image," said the president. "Sometimes I just want to get up and go to Hawaii and never come back."

Just then the door opened and a well-dressed couple walked into the room. The woman was in a formal eastern dress and the man was in a dark suit. They happily shook hands with the president, who met them in his usual friendly manner. The couple then left the room. The president was puzzled by their leaving.

"Did they not come with you?"

"I don't know these people," said Adnan.

"Forgive me, but they are strangers to me."

"Only four of us came to see you, Mr. President," added Hisaab Khan.

My mouth was full but I shrugged my shoulders to indicate to the president that I did not know the couple. The president was not amused. "Give me a minute please," he said picking up the phone next to him. It was a proper heavy phone out of the eighties that suited the majesty of this powerful room. "Yes, please send the head of security."

The head of security was soon in the room and the president was questioning him about the friendly couple. "I am concerned about people walking into a highly secure area of the White House without proper authorization."

"But, sir," said the security official, "they knew the password so we had to let them in."

"What is the password?"

"The password is *I don't know.*"

"Okay, you need to change that."

After this small incident, the president came back to his chair and Adnan continued the serious conversation.

"Mr. President, I have a couple of suggestions on how traffic can be better managed on our highways."

The President was intrigued and leaned forward.

"How can we do that? Please share your ideas."

"As you know that on the highways we have the right lane for exits, the fast lane, the HOV lane for car pooling. And on some streets we even have lanes for cyclists."

"Yes," said the president. "What else can we do?"

"We should add a swimmer's lane to the highway. This could be filled with water and people will have the opportunity to swim to work."

The president smiled at the idea and said, "The idea does hold water."

"Yes, and rain could replenish the swimming lane."

"That is an interesting thought. Tell you what—I'll float this idea with the Department of Transportation."

"Swimming is very good for the health," emphasized Adnan.

"I will send your proposal to the Department of Transportation and if the idea sinks in we might see some changes."

The meeting was going well. Adnan made some more suggestions. "Mr. President the countries of the world spend a total of one trillion dollars every year on defense. We do this out of fear. And whom do we fear? Is it lions or cheetahs or alligators? No. We spend out of fear of one another. I suggest an international conference where all the world leaders should meet and decide that for twenty-five years we are not going to attack one another."

"I like your idea. By declaring world peace for twenty-five years we would save twenty-five trillion dollars."

"Exactly!" said Adnan. "This can be invested in infrastructure projects in America and all over the world. A bullet train that moves happily through all the countries in the world."

"Such a train would have to be bulletproof, but your idea has merit," said the president. "Tell me why are you planning to leave on this ship you call the ARK? You have announced your launch date for the thirteenth of November."

"Yes," said Adnan.

"I want you to call off your plan for three reasons." The President loved to count. "Number one, there is plenty to be discovered right here in America. Start your journey at an organic grocery store. I still don't know half the crazy things they have in their salad bar. You could explore that."

Maaf Karna, Hisaab Khan, and I nodded in agreement, but Adnan simply listened to the president, who continued his counting.

"Number two, your ARK is facing problems with security. There are reports that riots break out regularly on your ship." The president walked over to his desk and showed us large black and white picture of the ARK taken from a satellite. It was an image of people fighting and throwing chairs at each other. "We have intelligence reports that when you tried to order pizza, the residents of your ARK could not agree on the toppings. The veggie lovers fought it out with the meat lovers. Some were thrown overboard. In the end the only thing they could agree upon were the bread sticks. Think about it. This can only get worse."

And then the president gave his last reason why Adnan should cancel the launch of the ARK. "And number three, you have no fuel."

"Will he kill himself?"

O N THE twelfth of November, the excitement level peaked. Reporters from all over the world were now camped on the pier below us. A reporter spoke excitedly into the camera, describing the tense situation:

Adnan Raheem Khan, leader of the Desi League, has created a living city on a massive ship that he calls the ARK. He has claimed that the ARK will launch into the open sea tomorrow at six a.m. Experts doubt that this can happen because this ARK that you see behind me has no fuel—no oil, coal, wood, or solar panels. We have also learned that bets are being placed on this matter. Thousands of gamblers have bet against the ARK moving. Our investigations reveal that Adnan Raheem Khan has also placed a hundred-thousand-dollar bet in favor of the ARK launching. It is confirmed that odds against the ARK launching are a million to one.

At another area on the pier, *Hi There News* had created a discussion panel. Seated at this panel were distinguished experts and academics. Among them was a man who had obtained a PhD in the science of movement. He was a born academic. At his birth, his parents had given him the name Doctor. After obtaining his PhD he was now called Doctor Doctor which boosted his self-esteem and made him an established authority on all matters related to transportation. He had a large bald head and he smoked a pipe. In his beige, well-pressed trousers and black turtleneck sweater, he was the framed picture of seriousness. Even the journalist who interviewed him did so with the deepest respect.

"Doctor Doctor, you are an established authority on the science of movement. You have taken a keen interest in the ARK and recently authored, *Why It Won't Move.* Do you think that there is even a tiny chance the size of a baby bacterium's toe that this ship will launch?"

The professor blew smoke into the air from the corner of his mouth in a most sophisticated manner as the world had seen him do in documentaries.

"Absolutely not! This ship has no source of power. We know for a fact that the ship has no fuel oil, no coal, not even chopped wood that they can burn to create steam. Beneath this ship are large propellers that resemble ceiling fans. These are connected to an engine. For the ship to move forward these propellers must receive power from the engine so that they can rotate at great speed and propel the ship forward. Since there is nothing to power the engine, we can safely assume that the propellers will not rotate; hence, this so-called ARK is staying here!" He banged his fist on the table to emphasize the word "here." The world heard him. He then let out a laugh that was the first cousin of mockery and the nephew of sarcasm. "They will probably turn this ship into a restaurant of some kind and serve fish sandwiches." He laughed again never opening his mouth to release the laughter but allowing it to escape through his nose in small clouds of tobacco smoke.

The reporter summarized the rest. "So there you have it, ladies and gentlemen. Doctor Doctor, the greatest authority on the subject of movement, has rejected the possibility of a launch. We now remain here to see how the leader of the Desi League, Adnan Raheem Khan, will handle the disgrace that is sure to fall on him tomorrow at dawn. Will he kill himself? Anything's possible, so please stay tuned."

Along with the media and the panel of experts, thousands of regular people were gathered. Because of budget cuts in the space programs the people had gathered here to see the massive ARK instead while eating cotton candy and taking pictures.

On the evening of the twelfth of November, Adnan ordered all residents of the ARK to be in bed by ten. The ARK launch was scheduled for the next morning at six. We slept peacefully knowing that this whole business about the launch was going to come to an end.

The next morning at five thirty we woke up to the booming sound of drums. Adnan's voice echoed on all speakers. He asked us to gather on the main deck. He stood on the deck, loud speaker in hand, in his captain's hat, dark-blue jacket, crisp white shirt, and well-pressed khakis.

"Out there," he said pointing to the huge crowd of reporters and spectators gathered on the dock, "they are eating cotton candy and the world is watching you. I ask only one thing from you today. No matter what happens, just be yourselves." We clapped for him and everyone liked the speech because it was short.

At six when the sun was rising and the ocean was ablaze with light, turning into an orange-pinkish color, Adnan gave the signal. A man blew into a trumpet announcing the launch.

"They sounded the launch trumpet," shouted a reporter on the docks.

"How dare they pretend to be so confident when failure awaits them?" shouted Doctor Doctor.

Adnan remained calm. He spoke firmly into the loudspeaker. For the first time the ARK was silent in anticipation. I was so nervous I could hear my nose breathing. Adnan Raheem Khan, our great leader, took complete command.

"Is Engine Room One ready?"

"Yes, sir," I shouted.

"Forgive me, but yes it is," said Maaf Karna.

"One hundred percent," said Hisaab Khan.

As leading members of the Desi League, we had designed three engine rooms. They had been easy to design, because all they contained was a long table that ran across each room. Following Adnan's instructions, we had placed chairs on both sides of each table. In front of every chair, the scientific team had placed jumper cables that we use to start cars. We were told that these cables were all connected to the engine of the ship. And that was it. No batteries, no solar panel, no fuel.

"Engine Room One, organize!" shouted Adnan. Hundreds of Desis rushed into the engine room numbered one. They took their places on the chairs. Each Desi faced the other across the table and held the electrodes of the jumper cable in their hands.

"Engine Room One, activate."

At this command every Desi sitting at the table made eye contact with the Desi sitting opposite him. As is a well-known fact, when a Desi looks at another Desi he emits negative energy. We see this in the malls, and our colorful history of conflict on the subcontinent is evidence of this. By placing Desis on chairs facing each other, each Desi experienced an extreme dislike. This negative energy was absorbed by the electrodes as negative particles or electrons. Electricity was created and flowed into the engine. The propellers attached to the hull of the ARK came to life! With a great sound the water around the ARK was bubbling. We were edging away from the docks.

"We are witnessing a modern miracle! The ARK is moving!" shouted a reporter.

Doctor Doctor dropped the pipe from his mouth and ran toward the ARK as it moved toward the sea.

"How can I be wrong? I have never made a mistake! How are they doing this?"

But our great leader, Adnan, was not done yet.

"Let's give them a show they will never forget. Engine Room Two, activate!"

"Sir, are you sure about this?" said a crew member. Engine Room Two is only to be used for emergencies. Can we handle this much power generation?"

"Now is the time," said Adnan. "Engine Room Two, are you ready?"

"We are most ready," came the collective reply of a hundred female voices.

The powerful Engine Room Two was controlled completely by women. Just like the first room, Engine Room Two had a long table with chairs. Sitting on these chairs, electrodes in hand, facing each other were a hundred women. But this was no random gathering. Adnan and the scientific team had made each woman sit opposite her mother-in-law. And when they looked into each other's eyes they recalled angry incidents, passive-aggressive comments, words of unwanted advice, compliments that first sounded sincere but contained criticisms. It all came back to them and flowed as negatively charged particles into the electrodes. So intimate was Adnan's involvement in this engine room that leading this effort was his own mother, who sat across from Naureen, his very angry wife. As they locked stares, negatively charged particles flowed from their hands into the engine. The ARK, now powered by an intensity the world had never witnessed, lurched forward and glided toward the open sea.

The people on the pier were frantically taking pictures. The gamblers were angry and one who was philosophical about the whole thing commented, "It is as if we are losing a part of ourselves." Doctor Doctor, a strict rationalist, lost his scientific reserve and got down on his knees crying.

"Look at the ARK move! It is driven by some kind of magic!"

In a way he was right. The magic was within us.

The ARK was now gliding at a steady pace. But Adnan was not done yet. "Engine Room Three, activate."

Engine Room Three was filled with religious people. Muslims, Hindus, Sikhs, Christians, Shias, and Sunnis were arranged so that followers of opposing religions and sects faced each other. They all wore their respective hats and holy colors that they considered more important than goodwill. As these religious men made eye contact, a thousand years of suspicions were unleashed. All the theological arguments and insincere assumptions came to life in their minds. As Desis, they were very similar culturally, but this familiarity allowed them to identify differences that other nations might have overlooked. The negative energy generated from this room still remains a world record, and it was said that if the sun had feelings it would have been extremely jealous of Engine Room Three. The massive ARK leaped into the air with this surge of negative energy.

Adnan Raheem Khan truly was our great leader. He had figured out that the more similar we are, the more we hate each other. And these feelings he had turned into renewable energy.

I was on the deck at this moment and still remember the wind and spray hitting my face as the ARK zoomed ahead. As we gained speed, I looked back and saw the mainland getting smaller and smaller.

We had done it! By using our own feelings toward one another we left civilization far behind until it could no longer be seen.

The End

27899407R00149

Made in the USA
Charleston, SC
25 March 2014